OXFORD HANDBOOKS IN EMERGENCY MEDICINE

Series Editors R. N. Illingworth, C. E. Robertson, and M. Clancy

OXFORD HANDBOOKS IN EMERGENCY MEDICINE

This series has already established itself as the essential reference series for staff in A & E departments.

Each book begins with an introduction to the topic, including epidemiology where appropriate. The clinical presentation and the immediate practical management of common conditions are described in detail, enabling the casualty officer or nurse to deal with the problem on the spot. Where appropriate a specific course of action is recommended for each situation and alternatives discussed. Information is clearly laid out and easy to find—important for situations where swift action may be vital.

Details on when, how, and to whom to refer patients are covered, as well as the information required at referral, and what this information is used for. The management of the patient after referral to a specialist is also outlined.

The text of each book is supplemented with checklists, key points, clear diagrams illustrating practical procedures, and recommendations for further reading.

The Oxford Handbooks in Emergency Medicine are an invaluable resource for every member of the A & E team, written and edited by clinicians at the sharp end.

Legal Problems in Emergency Medicine

Alan Montague
Barrister, Consultant in Emergency Medicine,
Southmead Hospital, Westbury on Trym, Bristol

with the assistance of

Andrew Hopper
Solicitor, Consultant, Cartwrights Adams & Black, Cardiff

Oxford • New York • Melbourne • Toronto
OXFORD UNIVERSITY PRESS
1996

Oxford University Press, Walton Street, Oxford OX2 6DP

Oxford   New York
Athens   Auckland   Bangkok   Bombay
Calcutta   Cape Town   Dar es Salaam   Delhi
Florence   Hong Kong   Istanbul   Karachi
Kuala Lumpur   Madras   Madrid   Melbourne
Mexico City   Nairobi   Paris   Singapore
Taipei   Tokyo   Toronto
and associated companies in
Berlin   Ibadan

Oxford is a trade mark of Oxford University Press

Published in the United States
by Oxford University Press Inc., New York

A catalogue record for this book is available from the British Library

Library of Congress Cataloging in Publication Data
ISBN 0 19 262496 2 (Pbk)
ISBN 0 19 262497 0 (Hbk)

Typeset by Footnote Graphics, Warminster, Wilts
Printed in Great Britain by
Biddles Ltd, Guildford & King's Lynn

Contents

vi • Contents

Introduction

Law and medicine are unlike disciplines. The practice of medicine is based on direct logic yet requires the application of many assumptions and traditions. Law uses an inductive logic and is concerned with interpretation of the language of actual utterances, either written or spoken.

Bridging this gap is a constant process of interpretation. Any statement of English Law is itself an interpretation and cannot provide a set of rules to cover every situation. Despite the modern increase of litigation there are few cases that make new law. For the many hypothetical situations covered here, it is rare to find a case decided by a higher court on similar facts. Much of this book consists of guidance through the authorities to show well-founded law which can be relied and acted upon. Some is necessarily the authors' opinion. It is made plain when this is the case.

This book is divided into a practical section and a reference section. Part 1 is guidance for some situations which doctors and others practising emergency medicine may find difficult. Some will be common, others not. Some will develop rapidly, others can be contemplated at leisure.

There is overlap between the two sections but they serve different purposes. Each part of the first section is self-contained and direct. Part 2 is a statement of the current law of England and Wales concerning these topics. It is unsafe to make projections that 'foreign' law, including Scottish Law, will be similar.

The practical section—Part 1

Each topic should be read in its entirety. The law gives few short answers! The chapter and section headings are self-explanatory and are listed at the beginning. Each chapter is complete. However, if issues of consent arise as they often do, it will be helpful first to read Chapter 3 (Obtaining consent).

1

The reference section—Part 2

The reference section is further reading and explanation. It follows the traditional division of medico-legal topics. Law is a more mature discipline than medicine. Lawyers, being less arrogant, have always required authority for every statement whereas we doctors can still boldly aver things and have people believe us. Therefore this section has legal references, especially where the law is dynamic or is uncertain.

Legal notes and references

Most legal notes in this book are explanations of or quotations from significant court decisions or Acts of Parliament. They are followed by their precise legal reference which pinpoints their location in a law library. They are included for the unremarkable purpose of justifying statements of law in the text. This sort of book cannot be trusted unless it is authoritative and can be verified. We have not expanded upon many references for reasons of space and continuity but they are often interesting in their own right and worth looking up, both for the stories they contain and as the actual source of the law.

Looking up cases and statutes

The best place is a university or college law library. The librarians will quickly teach visitors to decode legal references or citations according to rules outlined below.

Cases

Decided cases, in the higher courts, are reported in the established law reports as well as in some newspapers and specialist journals. The former are normally scrutinized by the judges in the case and are more authoritative. They are kept and referred to as bound volumes by year or part of a year. Law reports in newspapers such as *The Times* and in legal journals can be cited in court if written by qualified lawyers. Case references are written in a conventional shorthand form, explained below.

An example of a citation and its meaning:
DPP v. *Majewski* [1977] AC 443, [1976] 2 All ER 142 (HL)

DPP v. *Majewski*
Cases are known by the names of the parties to the case. In this instance the prosecutor was the Director of Public Prosecutions and the defendant Mr Majewski.

[1977]
Square brackets indicate the year the report was published. Alternative round brackets indicate the year the case was decided.

AC

Short for the name of the series of reports, written on the spine of the volume; in this instance 'Appeal Cases'.

443
The page at which the report begins.

[1976] 2 All ER 142
The case was in fact reported twice, the second reference being to page 142 of Volume 2 of the All England Reports of 1976. The volume number, if necessary, comes after the year.

(HL)
The report is of the findings of the Appellate Committee of the House of Lords.

Statutes

Finding a statute or Act of Parliament is easy since they are listed in order of date. Modern statutes have a name and a year (AD) and are divided into sections and subsections. Some have well known nicknames, e.g. 'PACE' for the Police and Criminal Evidence Act 1984.

Statutory instruments

These are regulations made by a minister under authority of an Act of Parliament. An example is the 1985 Misuse of Drugs Regulations made under the Misuse of Drugs Act 1971. They are cited by year and serial number.

Casebooks

These consist of extracts from cases and statutes, intended for law students. They are cheap and self-contained. *Medical Law* by Kennedy and Grubb (2nd edn, 1994 Butterworths) is recommended.

Gender

The authors recognize that most uses in this book of the word 'he' could be replaced by 'she' or 'he or she' without altering the meaning. 'He' is generally used alone for economy of style. When we intended to mean the male sex alone we have endeavoured to make it apparent. We do not intend to give offence to women.

Part 1

Practical problems

CHAPTER 1

Avoiding trouble

- The problem—the risk of being sued 7 • The solution—how to avoid it 8

Key points

1 Be polite to and open with patients.
2 Keep careful notes.
3 Know your limitations.
4 There is a legal duty to care adequately for every patient who comes to an open emergency department.
5 Join a defence society.

The problem—the risk of being sued

The term 'defensive medicine' implies medical practice directed to protect the doctor from being sued rather than care of a patient. In particular it infers excessive and unnecessary investigation. Of course, good lawyers reassure us, this is quite unnecessary for as long as we act in accordance with a responsible body of medical opinion we cannot successfully be sued. Unfortunately this is not the invariable interpretation by hospital management and defence unions. They are known to pay off smaller claims whether meritorious or not.

And the fires are fuelled by those among our number who may be tempted, perhaps out of sympathy, to side unduly with a plaintiff. Their medical reports are frequently swallowed without challenge. This goes beyond giving fair and just compensation for injury. Most patients are honest but among the millions will be a few of the alternative persuasion. When they make their effortless trouble it generates anxiety and a sense of outrage. Most of them will obtain legal aid and many will go on to win a prize. The following remarks are not aimed to deprive the victims of our mistakes of their proper compensation. On the contrary they encourage good practice with incidental protection from dirty tricks.

The solution—How to avoid it

Professional conduct

Good professional conduct requires simple good manners and polite affability. Suing is one way of getting even with the arrogant and condescending.

Communication

Show absolute openness and frankness over factual matters with patients and their relatives, especially after errors occur or when results are poor. This does not require an admission of negligence. Those who suspect something has gone wrong will go to great lengths to discover what it was. Evasiveness will inflame their distress and sharpen their curiosity. Before embarking on any procedure or investigation explain it in plain words and be sure to be understood. Make liberal use of the consent form and follow its instructions.

Evidence

Make careful and clear notes. It may be the patient's only case and certainly his only one involving litigation; it is one of thousands for the casualty officer and therefore the notes will in time represent his entire knowledge of the incident. If it comes to court the notes are one of the few impartial indicators to distinguish a careful from a slapdash doctor. Use only simple, clear, and unambiguous language.

When a complaint comes to light it is in order to make subsequent additional notes but they must be properly dated and identified as such. Alteration of existing notes will be recognized as dishonest.

Referral

Know and respect your limitations. Never pretend skills or knowledge you do not possess. When in doubt refer to seniors

At the trial a High Court Judge decided that an obstetrician had pulled too hard for too long on obstetric forceps causing brain damage. He had in fact abandoned a trial of forceps and proceeded to caesarean section after pushing back the head. In his notes he had used the word 'disimpacted' to describe this latter manoeuvre. The whole case seems to have turned on this one word in the notes. Doctors of course know what it means in a surgical context. The Judge preferred the ordinary meaning of the word however, implying that the head had been 'impacted' by excessive force. Long and formidably expensive appeals first to the Court of Appeal then to the House of Lords established that he had not pulled too hard for too long. One word had been misunderstood by the first judge. Beware of words!

(*Whitehouse* v. *Jordan* [1981] 1 All ER 267)

in the department or others in the hospital with more expertise. Record that referral. Asking the opinion of one equally or less experienced such as a houseman will not protect a casualty officer.

Appropriate investigations

Take a proper history, perform a careful examination, and record both. Consider the differential diagnosis and consider which if any may be an accident or an emergency. The appropriate investigations are those that confirm or exclude emergency conditions. These must be ordered and the fact recorded; this is not the time to spare the hospital's budget. However, any other investigations should be considered as defensive medicine and not done. It is irrelevant that hospital managers and the defence unions might choose to criticize you. If you practise good clinical medicine you have no reason to be abashed and are unlikely to be successfully sued.

Inappropriate attenders

However emergency physicians interpret their role, there will inevitably be some customers that fit this designation (or the more politically correct 'primary care'). These people do not have problems needing urgent treatment. Some of them think they have, many have the mistaken belief that emergency departments are 'better' than family doctors and many are insufficiently industrious to go and see them. While their proper course is to consult their family doctor, identifying them may not be all that simple. It must be clearly understood that the hospital and its staff owe a duty of care to anybody who comes to an open emergency department.

> For example three workmen came to an open emergency department, suddenly vomiting after drinking tea and appearing ill with what later proved to be arsenic poisoning. The duty nurse saw them and telephoned the casualty officer who, from his bed, said they should go home and call in their own doctors. They followed this advice and died. The court held that coming to an open emergency department creates a legal relationship between patients and the hospital so that the nurse and the doctor were under a duty of care to the deceased.
>
> (*Barnett* v. *Chelsea and Kensington Hospital Management Committee* [1969] 1 QB 428, [1968] 1 All ER 1068 (QBD))

Every patient must therefore be seen by an experienced member of staff who should carefully and skilfully establish whether or not they have a condition which is an emergency. In every case a duty is owed them and so, if discharging them from the emergency department without treatment they must be properly advised as to their next steps and this advice recorded. The standard of care required by the law is a medical one, even if a nurse discharges the patient.

Defence societies

These institutions have honourable histories and high standards. Since the NHS provided professional indemnity their role and cost have diminished. The following points are in favour of belonging.

(a) They are now cheap for the doctor with minimal private work.
(b) They provide telephone advice on legal matters.
(c) They provide a safety net of professional indemnity insurance covering any extra duties the doctor may do including attending emergencies outside the hospital and writing reports.

CHAPTER 2

Emergency department discipline

• **Notes 12** • **Audit 15** • **Guidelines, protocols, and procedures 16**

Key points

1 Good notes imply good practice.
2 Subsequent additions to notes must be identified as such.
3 Audit is a sound practice but the fact it is practised will not affect individual cases of medical negligence. Liability attaches to individuals, not the team.
4 Documents created for audit purposes may be used in evidence.
5 The standards of practice accepted by the courts are the same throughout the country and cannot be reduced by local rules or guidelines.
6 Guidelines and procedures may be evidence of a professional standard but do not set that standard.
7 Nurses doing medical work are judged by medical standards.

Notes

One way of valuing an institution is to consider its cost and what it produces. An emergency department's only enduring 'product', beside its treated patients, is its notes. It is important therefore that these reflect the true standard of care and are not slipshod. In medical negligence litigation clinical notes are scrutinized in untiring detail by the parties, their lawyers, and the judges. Good note keeping habits reduce the risk of unfairly losing in this most expensive game. The following suggestions may be helpful.

Standardized format

All clinical notes should contain in proper order:
- history
- physical findings
- investigations
- diagnosis
- treatment (if any)
- outcome or disposal.

Audit of notes

The content and quality of emergency department notes is a proper subject for audit and is found to be a valuable influence on new members of a department.[1]

Quips

Pejorative remarks, however justified, suggest a bad attitude. The busiest lawyers, who function an order of magnitude more leisurely than emergency department staff, cannot be expected to envisage the speed and activity of an emergency department and will draw broad and unjustified inferences from rapidly scribbled items of detail. The opposition will descend with glee upon 'NFN' or 'monosynaptic' and draw out an explanation in the witness box. Assume a patient will see everything written about him.

Referrals

These should be recorded, naming the person to whom a patient has been referred and the time of referral. If this is done routinely it will not give offence when it matters. In the absence of any record there is little the emergency department staff can do to avoid responsibility for any harm that may follow the failure of an in-patient specialist's junior to attend or to give proper advice.

Nursing notes

If a doctor agrees with nursing or other notes and does not wish to repeat them he must specifically refer to them and incorporate them (e.g. 'agree with triage note overleaf').

Diagrams

These should be labelled and include dimensions.

Photographs

Clinical photographs are more informative if they contain a centimetre scale in the picture and show details of the patient's identity, the time, and date and are referred to in the notes.

Labelling of attached documents

Continuation sheets, electrocardiograms, laboratory results, letters, photographs, observation charts, et cetera must be labelled with the patient's name and the date. Never rely on sheets of paper remaining identifiable by being bound or stapled together.

Trouble anticipated

Sometimes there may be a hint of trouble ahead. If so, it is wise to have a witness present during the remainder of the consultation who should sign the notes as a true record of what happened. Fuller than normal notes may be worthwhile. Notes need not only be sufficiently full, they must also be believed.

Subsequent alteration of notes

An attempt to hide or alter what was written will be seen in a poor light and will appear as shabby and dishonest as it is. It will discredit a doctor or nurse as a witness and lead to disciplinary action. On the other hand it is proper to make subsequent additions to notes if this is done openly. No objection can be made to drawing a line under existing notes, marking the present date and time and then writing and signing further notes.

Retaining Notes

The limitation period, after which litigation is forbidden, is three years in personal injury cases. There are exceptions to this rule, for instance the period does not begin to run until the victim becomes aware of the connection between the wrong treatment and the harm it caused.[2] Therefore the hospital should keep clinical notes for considerably longer than 3 years. Be cautious of cases where there is conflict of interest, especially where others may wish to transfer blame away from themselves. It is wise to copy all notes and investigations and keep copies for security against loss or forgery. There is more than one occurrence recorded in the law reports of hospital documents conveniently being lost.

Audit

Clinical audit is an increasing pastime of NHS staff. A department practising clinical audit is likely to be safer and more efficient. By regular assessment of the process of care, safety is enhanced with reduced risk of litigation. Audit is perhaps analogous to the routine safety checking of a vehicle or machine although this analogy can be taken too far at this early stage of its entrenchment into medical practice.

Legal effect

The fact that a team audits its work may be evidence of good practice and of concern for standards. There is no legal requirement to audit. Medical negligence cases are at present about the particular care of an individual judged according to the legal standard (see Chapter 11). They are not concerned with the whole system of care or its usual achievements. The law may be changing in this respect; a patient has just successfully sued a health authority for failing to provide a safe system of care (see Chapter 6). If this legal principle is taken up by other judges, audit will acquire a legal importance of its own.

Audit documents not exempt from discovery

If errors and negligent acts which come to light during clinical audit are documented and such documents kept they will be subject to the process of discovery, a pre-trial procedure in which the existence of all documents relating to a case must be disclosed to the opposing party. Audit documents are not exempt from this including audio and videotapes and machine traces. Some hospital teams prefer to hold audit meetings behind closed doors and not to retain documents concerning specific patients.

> A department makes and keeps video recordings of trauma resuscitation, purely for audit purposes. After discharge from hospital a patient sues, alleging his neurological injury is due to errors in his case. Before trial the hospital will have to declare the existence of all relevant documents including the tapes.

Guidelines, Protocols, and Procedures

Anyone attempting to practise medicine or nursing in the 1990s will be aware of the proliferation of 'protocols' and other written guidance appearing from all directions. They already cause concern over 'cookbook medicine' and inhibition of clinical freedom. What is their legal effect? This question can be divided into:

(1) What is the legal status of guidelines?
(2) Is a practitioner liable in negligence if he obeys them?
(3) Is he liable if he ignores them?
(4) Can the writer of them be liable in negligence for acts done in obedience to them?

The legal status of guidelines

Administrative
Performance standards set by NHS purchasers or 'Patients' Charters' are almost certainly of no legal effect. It is less easy

to dismiss management guidelines for the appropriate use of limited resources. This is a complex area of debate. Judges recognize that hospital managers have to juggle with limited funds. The judges will not interfere with their allocations unless they are plainly illegal or outrageously unreasonable (see Chapter 6). It is up to a practitioner to insist on his professional standards and he is bound to treat each patient according to those standards by whatever means are at his disposal. If the means are insufficient, he must make this known to the hospital's management.

Clinical
On the other hand clinical guidelines set out standards of care or safe working practices and procedures. These have a variable influence and authority in law depending on who wrote them and for whom.

The standard of care expected of a professional person is an independent one, imposed by the judiciary. It is 'that of the ordinary skilled man, exercising and professing to have that special skill'. This is known as the *Bolam* test. If a case comes to court that standard is a question of fact to be decided by the judge in each case. He must balance and resolve conflicting views of experts called to assist the court. Some expert's views will be preferred to others.

To escape liability in negligence, it is enough for a defendant to show he acted in accordance with a body of competent professional opinion. The opinion need not be that of the majority of the profession.

In deciding the standard in legal proceedings, guidelines and procedures may be referred to as evidence of a professional standard.

It follows that guidelines will occupy a point on a scale of authority depending on the professional standing and experience of those who wrote them and on their degree of deliberation and agreement in doing so.

There is, in general, a tendency of the courts to be influenced by accepted codes of practice, whether governmental in origin or from a professional body. National bodies of repute that put out guidance for the profession will almost certainly embrace a responsible and competent body of opinion.

An example of a guideline accepted as the profession's standard is found in Lord Goff's remarks in *Airedale NHS Trust* v. *Bland* where he said '. . . if a doctor treating a (persistent vegetative state) patient acts in accordance with the medical practice being evolved by the Medical Ethics Committee of the British Medical Association he will be acting with the benefit of guidance from a responsible and a competent body of relevant professional opinion, as required by the *Bolam* test'.

(*Airedale NHS Trust* v. *Bland* [1993] 1 All ER 821 at p. 872; The *Bolam* test is discussed in Chapter 11)

Is a practitioner liable in negligence if he obeys them?

All guidelines must be examined critically and not followed blindly. Guidelines should only be followed if they recommend practices that are in accordance with 'a responsible and competent body of relevant professional opinion', not otherwise.[3]

Is a practitioner liable if he ignores them?

A practitioner who ignores guidelines may irritate colleagues but it will not lead to liability in negligence unless the treatment is not in accordance with 'a responsible and competent body of relevant professional opinion'. Therefore, as far as the law of negligence is concerned, clinical freedom is not curtailed by guidelines.

Can the writer of guidelines be liable?

If the advice of a senior is sought by a junior and acted upon and harm results, the fault will lie with the senior (see Chapter 11). The same rule must apply to standing instructions in writing as applies to spoken advice. Local guidance which causes junior staff to give treatment not in accordance with 'a responsible and competent body of relevant professional opinion' will render the writer of the guideline liable for resulting harm.

Local guidelines: effect on the junior who obeys

Local guidelines and procedures may be drawn up for the guidance of junior staff to indicate a consultant's preferences. If they satisfy the *Bolam* test there is no more to discuss. If there is doubt as to their reliability then, provided they are not grossly unreasonable, they probably place the junior in the position he would have been in if he had asked his senior's advice and acted on it.

The effects of guidelines on juniors' practice was explored in *Early* v. *Newham HA*. In that case a patient had suffered a terrifying experience during induction of anaesthesia. Intubation was unsuccessful and she woke up still paralysed by suxamethonium. The anaesthetist SHO had correctly obeyed local instructions to: 'maintain cricoid pressure, ventilate with oxygen, not persist with attempts at intubation, turn the patient on the side, call for help . . . allow patient to wake up.'

The plaintiff alleged the procedural guidance was faulty and flawed. Her anaesthetist expert advised the court that 'no reasonably competent medical authority would have condoned this drill'. The deputy High Court Judge found that the anaesthetic drill had been properly considered by the division of anaesthesia at the hospital which had balanced the risks involved and considered the risk of transient terror to be outweighed by the risks of hypoxia or aspiration. The health authority's guidance had therefore been reasonable and competent.

(*Early* v. *Newham HA* [1994] 5 Med LR 214)

The special position of nurses

There isn't one! A nurse is a professional person like any other. The practice of medicine does not require a medical degree in this country. But whatever is done to a patient, and whoever does it, he or she is entitled to expect a proper standard of care. A patient is not required to make allowances for anybody's lack of expertise (see Chapter 11).

Nurses are now doing tasks once done only by doctors such as minor surgery and treating and discharging patients. In the areas of practice traditionally limited to doctors the responsible and competent body of opinion must be medical opinion. Accordingly many hospitals' administrations have drawn up local procedures for nursing staff to follow in performing these tasks without medical supervision.

Guidelines and procedures have similar legal effects on nurses as on junior doctors. Provided the procedures themselves are in accordance with a responsible and competent body of medical opinion, nurses will be safe from litigation if they follow them with skill and care.

An employing hospital will be liable to compensate patients injured by the clinical errors of any staff that occur in the course of their employment. A further effect of guidelines and procedures is to confirm that nurses following them are indeed acting in the course of their employment.

End notes

1. Quality Assurance in Guy's Hospital Accident and Emergency Department. Miller, E., Montague, A., Crone, P., Kirby, N. G. (1992). *Health Trends*, **24**, 38–40.
2. Limitation Act 1980 sections 11(4) and 14.
3. for example: Guidelines for initial management after head injury in adults. Suggestions from a group of neurosurgeons (1984). *BMJ*, **228**, 983–5.

CHAPTER 3

3 Obtaining consent

Key points

1. Nothing whatever can be done to anyone without consent or a court order except where the legal doctrine of necessity is invoked.

2. 'Necessity' can only be invoked where the patient is

(a) unable to understand what he is to consent to (through unconsciousness, severe mental disorder or immaturity) and

(b) the proposed treatment is necessary to 'save life, ensure improvement, or prevent deterioration in health'.

3. A valid refusal of treatment has to be observed however irrational.

4. Children can themselves consent to treatment if they have reached '*Gillick* awareness' which means having achieved a sufficient understanding and intelligence to understand fully what is proposed.

5. For a child who has not become '*Gillick* aware' consent can only be given by one with parental responsibility[1] or the court.

6. Good medical practice requires consultation with parents and other carers whenever possible.

This chapter is about obtaining valid consent in any circumstance. The law is outlined in Chapter 10. Consent does not

21

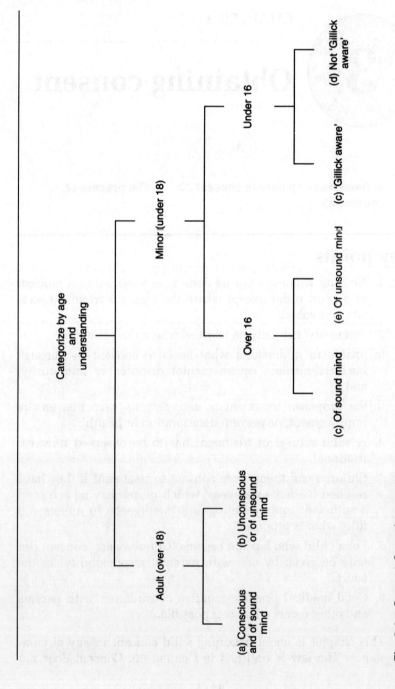

Fig. 3.1 • Stage 1 Capacity to consent.

require any formality, it can be verbal or even a gesture, such as baring a limb for an injection, but it is sensible to demand a signature for anything invasive, complex, risky, or involving sedation or general anaesthesia. This is to ensure there is evidence of the consent. In difficult situations, such as in obtaining parental consent by telephone, it may be wise to have it witnessed.

Consent itself requires the nature of the procedure to be described in broad terms. Also, as part of the business of caring for a patient, a doctor must advise and explain the risks and benefits in suitable detail and be certain this is understood. The patient is then in a position to make a decision about his treatment in the light of adequate information and advice.

Obtaining consent is ordinarily straightforward, even in the emergency department. But occasionally there are patients suffering from youth, insanity, drink, mulishness, relatives, or a combination of these that can test the clinician and make him temporarily uncertain of his position. This practical method is for these and any other situations. It divides the process into two stages:

(1) assessment of legal capacity to consent

(2) the process of obtaining that consent.

Stage 1: Assessing capacity to consent

(The class of patient)
Begin by assigning the patient to one of five categories according to age and understanding; each has its own decision chain. The categories are:

(a) Adult: conscious and of sound mind
(b) Adult: unconscious or of unsound mind
(c) Minor: over 16 **or** '*Gillick* aware'
(d) Minor: under 16 and **not** '*Gillick* aware'
(e) Minor: over 16 but of unsound mind.

Definitions

'*Adult*' is a person over 18.

'*Minor*' is a person under 18 (also 'infant' or 'child').

'of sound mind'/'of unsound mind'
To satisfy the legal test a patient must be capable of broadly understanding the nature of the treatment. If he is not it will be due to impaired consciousness or very severe mental disorder. Thus even a paranoid schizophrenic who is 'sectionable' has been judged of sound mind for this purpose. The NHS Management Executive recommends (in Health Circular (90)22 'A guide to consent for examination or treatment') that the 'doctor in charge of the patient' interview the patient and form an opinion.

'Gillick aware'
A *'Gillick* aware' minor is capable of a full understanding and appreciation of the intended consequences of treatment and possible side effects and also the anticipated consequences of failure to treat. The degree of maturity required will depend on the treatment proposed. Simple treatment needs a simple decision requiring little maturity while complex matters require a mature mind. A minor patient is to be judged as an individual and not on chronological age. There is therefore no minimum age.

The NHS Management Executive (HC(90)22) recommends the doctor make a full note of the factors taken into account in assessing the child's capacity to give a valid consent. The law

---

The expression *'Gillick* aware' or *'Gillick* competent' arose from the important decision of the Appellate Committee of the House of Lords in the *'Gillick* case'.

Their lordships were asked if a doctor could provide a girl under 16 with contraception without the knowledge or consent of her parents. Their decision (that he could) was accompanied by an authoritative and far sighted review of the law of parental rights and consent by minors. They decided that the legal test is:

'Has he or she achieved a sufficient understanding and intelligence to enable him or her to understand fully what is proposed?'

(*Gillick* v. *West Norfolk and Wisbech AHA* [1986] AC 112, [1985] 3 All ER 402) (see also Chapter 10)

recognizes it is good clinical practice for a child to be seen with parents whenever possible; failing this, efforts should always be made to persuade a '*Gillick* aware' child that his or her parents be informed.

Stage 2: The process of consent

Having decided what sort of patient you have, follow the appropriate process below and in the flow charts.

Adult: conscious and of sound mind

Procedure

(1) Explain the broad nature of the treatment.

(2) Be sure the patient properly understands the purpose and risks of the treatment. How much information to give is a question of skill and clinical judgement.

(3) Be sure it is their own decision, free from the undue influence of others, especially in the case of prisoners, the institutionalized and where there is a strong religious influence.

If treatment is refused

Even if the refusal appears entirely irrational, treatment must not be given. This situation may demand particular care in explaining the importance of treatment. It is wise to have the explanation and refusal witnessed and recorded in the notes by doctor, witness and, if he will, the patient.

Exception: undue influence

If there are real doubts about the validity of the refusal because there has been undue influence by others and

(1) you believe the decision is being imposed on the patient **and**

(2) the situation is life-threatening or irreparable damage to health can be anticipated

then apply forthwith to the court for a declaration as to the lawfulness of the treatment. The consultant in charge of the patient should call the duty hospital manager and advise him to instruct the hospital's solicitors to proceed immediately.[2] He must indicate the degree of urgency of the treatment.

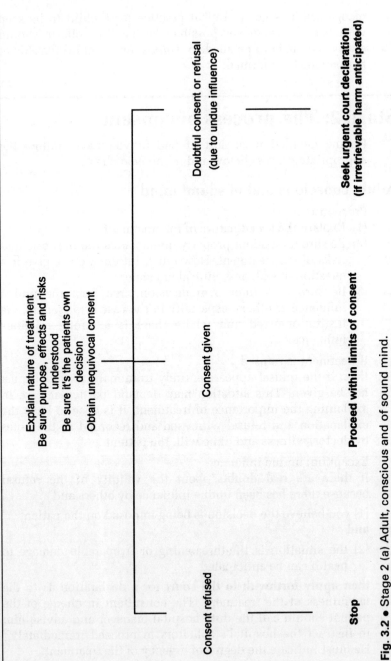

Explain nature of treatment
Be sure purpose, effects and risks understood
Be sure it's the patients own decision
Obtain unequivocal consent

Consent given

Consent refused

Doubtful consent or refusal
(due to undue influence)

Proceed within limits of consent

Stop

Seek urgent court declaration
(if irretrievable harm anticipated)

Fig. 3.2 • Stage 2 (a) Adult, conscious and of sound mind.

Adult: unconscious or unsound mind

No consent is possible and no-one can consent on his behalf. Can we nevertheless invoke the legal doctrine of necessity and treat him?

Procedure
(1) Consider and record in the notes:
Is the proposed treatment
(a) necessary to save life, ensure improvement or prevent deterioration in health?
(b) in accordance with established medical opinion?
(c) no more than reasonably required in the short term if the patient is expected to recover the capacity to consent to further treatment?
(2) If there is time,
(d) consult with next of kin or other relevant carers (if in doing this you learn of the patient's clear and unequivocal wishes, perhaps expressed in anticipation of these events, those wishes are binding)

If a,b,c, (and if time permits d) are fulfilled you may lawfully proceed without consent. This applies to any kind of treatment.

Minor: *Gillick* aware or over 16

Procedure
Treat as adult of sound mind (except as follows):
Refusal of consent
Those with parental responsibility[1] cannot override the wishes of a '*Gillick* aware' minor. However the decision whether a patient is sufficiently mature to be '*Gillick* aware' must take into account the complexity of the decision the young patient has to make. The most significant factor is likely to be the consequence, serious or otherwise, of not giving treatment. A minor patient would need to be particularly mature to be '*Gillick* aware' for the purpose of refusing life-saving treatment.

(2) Power of court,
The court has undoubted power to override the refusal of any minor. In cases of doubt, if there is time, an application to the court would always be possible.

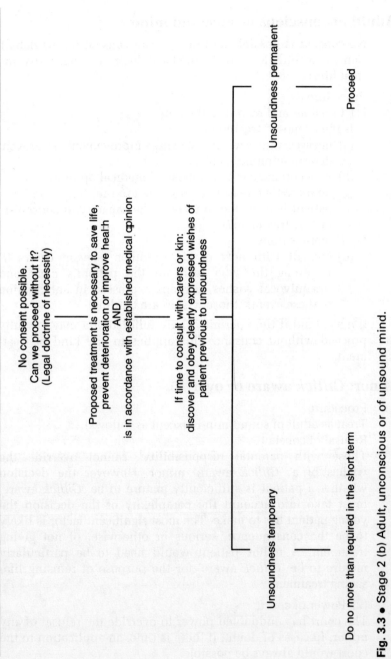

No consent possible.
Can we proceed without it?
(Legal doctrine of necessity)

Proposed treatment is necessary to save life,
prevent deterioration or improve health
AND
is in accordance with established medical opinion

If time to consult with carers or kin:
discover and obey clearly expressed wishes of
patient previous to unsoundness

Unsoundness permanent

Proceed

Unsoundness temporary

Do no more than required in the short term

Fig. 3.3 • Stage 2 (b) Adult, unconscious or of unsound mind.

E was an intelligent boy of 15 years, 9 months who was deteriorating rapidly with leukaemia. He was anaemic and thrombocytopaenic but he and his parents refused blood transfusion. Having interviewed him in hospital, Mr Justice Ward gave the hospital leave to give transfusions. He said: '. . . in my judgement (he) does not have a full understanding of the whole implication of what the refusal of that treatment involves.'

(*Re E (a minor) (wardship: medical treatment*) [1993] 1 FLR 386 at p. 391.)

A court may also override a minor's consent in certain circumstances and prevent treatment. Those with parental responsibility cannot override the minor's consent to treatment.

(3) Research and organ donation
No one under 18 can consent to be a research subject unless '*Gillick* aware' for this purpose but someone with parental responsibility (or the court) can do so on their behalf. Only a court can permit donation of a solid organ.

Minor: under 16 and not '*Gillick* aware'

Procedure
Obtain consent from one with parental responsibility. Discuss with them to:

(1) Explain the broad nature of the treatment
(2) Be sure the person consenting understands the purpose and risks of the treatment. How much information to give is a question of skill and clinical judgement.

No time to obtain consent:
Can we invoke the legal doctrine of necessity and treat without consent? Consider: is the proposed treatment:

(a) necessary to save life, ensure improvement or prevent deterioration in health?
(b) in accordance with established medical opinion?

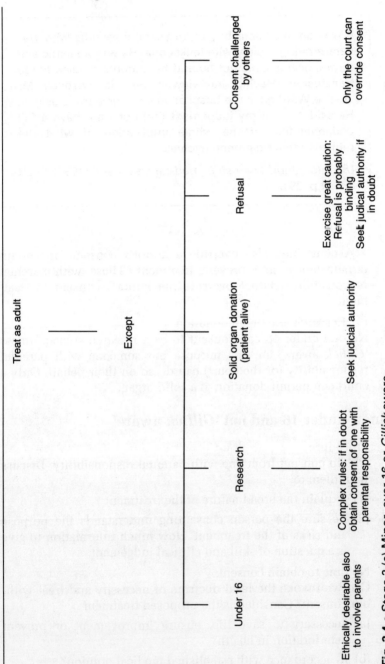

Fig. 3.4 • Stage 2 (c) Minor, over 16 or *Gillick* aware.

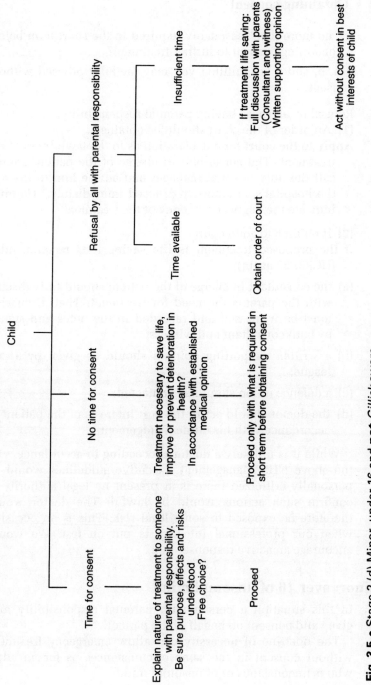

Fig. 3.5 • Stage 2 (d) Minor, under 16 and **not** *Gillick* aware.

(c) no more than reasonably required in the short term before obtaining consent to further treatment?

If a, b, and c are fulfilled you may lawfully proceed without consent.

Refusal by all those having parental responsibility:
(1) An order of the court should be obtained.
Apply to the court for a declaration as to the lawfulness of the treatment. The consultant in charge of the patient should call the duty hospital manager and advise him to instruct the hospital's solicitors to proceed immediately.[2] He must indicate the degree of urgency of the treatment.

(2) If no time to go to court:
If the proposed treatment is life saving it is recommended (HC(90)22 again):

(a) the consultant in charge of the patient should fully discuss with the parents the need for treatment. That discussion must be witnessed and recorded in the notes and signed by both consultant and witness;

(b) a written supporting opinion should be given by a colleague;

(c) a defence union should be contacted;

(d) the doctor should act in the best interests of the patient in accordance with his clinical judgement.

While it is unlikely a doctor proceeding in accordance with the above NHS Management Executive guidelines would be personally criticized there is at present no legal authority to confirm such actions would be lawful. The doctor would therefore be exposed to some legal risk. This is an occasion when our professional integrity is put on test. We would encourage an active response.

Minor: over 16 of unsound mind

In this situation a person with parental responsibility may give valid consent on behalf of the patient.

The doctrine of necessity can allow emergency treatment without consent in the same circumstances as for an adult who is unconscious or of unsound mind.

A person with parental responsibility can consent

Treat as under 16, not Gillick aware

Fig. 3.6 • Stage 2 (e) Minor, over 16 of unsound mind.

Examples

Adult of sound mind

An 18 year old man with AIDS has pneumonia. He refuses any treatment saying he wishes to die. His conversation is rambling and undisciplined. He is categorized with the help of Fig. 3.1. Can he understand the nature of the treatment being offered? If so he is an adult of sound mind.

Figure 3.2 is followed. The need for treatment, its risks and benefits, and the effect of non-treatment must be explained in suitable words. If he understands he may die and it is his own decision, with no one unduly influencing him, his refusal must be respected.

Adult of unsound mind

A frail elderly lady is brought to hospital by ambulance after collapsing in a nursing home. She is confused and cannot answer questions. She appears to be in worsening heart failure.

According to Fig. 3.1 she is an adult of unsound mind. Figure 3.3 reminds us that she cannot consent to treatment and no one can consent on her behalf. Without more information available it is certainly lawful to give emergency life-saving treatment.

Before she is treated her husband approaches you. He says she has poor quality of life, is in pain and, before this immediate illness, made it absolutely clear she wished no life-saving treatment if she became ill. In this situation it is lawful to respect her previously expressed wishes and not give treatment even if likely to succeed.

Minor under 16: '*Gillick* aware'

An intelligent 13 year old has lost a hand in a farm accident. It can probably be salvaged if done immediately. Efforts to contact his parents are unsuccessful. The theatre supervisor will not allow an operation to take place without 'a consent form'. A and E doctors are omniscient and so your advice is sought.

You look at the flow chart in Fig. 3.1. He is a minor under 16. Is he '*Gillick* aware'? This requires careful assessment but he probably satisfies the criteria and is mature enough to understand fully what is proposed. Figures 3.4 and 3.2 show that his consent can be obtained and is valid.

Before he can consent he becomes unconscious. He is clearly no longer '*Gillick* aware' or aware at all. It is now lawful to do what is necessary in the short term under the common law doctrine of necessity (*Re F, Chapter 10*).

Minor under 16: not '*Gillick* aware'[3]

A fifteen year old has taken a cocktail of drugs including a bottle of paracetamol. She is shouting hysterically and violently resists any examination. Her life is clearly at risk.

Following the pathway in Fig. 3.1 we conclude she is under 16, not '*Gillick* aware' for the purpose of refusing life-saving treatment (although she would have been '*Gillick* aware' to consent to treatment). Following Fig. 3.5 we telephone her mother and explain the importance and risks of any treatment. The patient can then lawfully be treated with the mother's consent.

End notes

1. Children Act 1989 lists persons and bodies with 'parental responsibility' (see Chapter 10, page 114)
2. The telephone number of the Royal Courts of Justice, through which the Official Solicitor, the Family Division duty officer and the duty High Court Judge can be contacted is: 0171 936 6000
3. See page 111

CHAPTER 4

Special patients with special problems

Jehovah's Witnesses

Key points

1. First consider whether the patient is competent to give or refuse consent (Chapter 3).

2. The refusal of blood transfusion by a legally competent person is binding but it must be his own decision, free of undue influence.

3. In the case of an incompetent adult (e.g. unconscious) the views of relatives are not binding. However, hospitals should obey a formal advance directive, made when competent, that no blood may be given.

4. If no person with parental responsibility will consent to an incompetent minor receiving blood, and his life or health is threatened, the High Court should be contacted immediately. If there is insufficient time for this a consultant must, on the proper criteria, decide and act.

Jehovah's witnesses are taught that it is wrong to receive elements of another's body including blood or its components. They usually refuse consent to it while accepting other medical treatment and technology such as plasma substitutes.

Judges have expressed respect for the sincerity with which such views are held while overriding them when necessary to protect children. The legal issues are not concerned with religious belief but the actual refusal of blood transfusion under life- or health-threatening circumstances. It should still be borne in mind that if Jehovah's Witnesses discover one of them has received blood he may be shunned and outcast. Always consider the possibility that he may in fact secretly wish to consent while concealing this from others of his faith.

This is one of many circumstances in which the general law pertaining to consent is applied. There are no special rules for people with these beliefs, the law is the same for everybody. This chapter contains advice concerning consent in a particular situation. It is supplementary to Chapter 3 (Obtaining consent) which must be read first.

Competent adult

The legal position is relatively straightforward. A competent adult, given clear and proper advice and making his own decision, is the master of his own body. His refusal must be respected. Those caring for him must still exercise proper skill within the limits he draws. A surgeon may be in a position to refuse to perform elective surgery under restrictive conditions or else choose a less radical operation, but in an emergency he must do the best he can.

The advice and refusal should be witnessed and recorded in the notes.

Competent adult under undue influence

It must be certain that the patient refuses of his own free will and not under the influence of others. It is proper to speak to him alone to be quite sure it is entirely his own decision. When in doubt the court's urgent help should be sought if the condition is life threatening or serious harm to health is likely (see Chapter 3).

Incompetent adult

A likely circumstance will be when a patient arrives who is not fully conscious. It is normally lawful to do what is necessary in the short term to save life or health. But what if his relatives say he is a Jehovah's Witness? By itself that is not sufficient to prevent a doctor invoking the doctrine of necessity and giving all the emergency treatment required. If, however, after consulting with relatives or carers it is clearly established that the patient has previously, while competent, made it unequivocally clear that he will not allow a blood transfusion under any circumstances, that refusal is binding. The decision is that of the patient, not his relatives. Such a conversation should be witnessed and recorded in the notes.

Previously expressed intentions (advance directives or 'living wills')

A signed card or other document may be found on a patient indicating an anticipatory choice. It will be binding if:

- he intended it to apply in these circumstances
- he was competent when he signed it

In a Canadian case (not binding English courts) a Mrs Malette was severely injured in a head-on collision. She was brought unconscious to the ER where Dr Shulman judged her in incipient shock and gave a volume expander. A nurse discovered a signed card in her purse which, translated, said:

'NO BLOOD TRANSFUSION

As one of Jehovah's witnesses with firm religious convictions, I request that no blood or blood products be administered to me under any circumstances. I fully realize the implications of this position, but I have resolutely decided to obey the Bible command 'Keep abstaining . . . from blood' (Acts 15:28, 29). However I have no religious objection to use the nonblood alternatives, such as Dextran, Haemaccel, PVP, Ringer's lactate, or saline solution.'

She showed it to Dr Shulman but the patient deteriorated in X-ray and he gave her blood on his own responsibility.

Mrs Malette survived, sued the doctor for battery, and won.

(*Malette* v. *Shulman* (1990) 67 DLR (4th) 321)

- he was not under undue influence
- he was aware of all the relevant risks.

In practice such a document must be carefully scrutinized and if a doctor judges it to be genuine he is bound to respect it.

Minor over 16 or '*Gillick* aware'

Such a patient will be in the same position as a competent adult except that persons with parental responsibility can, strictly, consent on his behalf if he refuses treatment. The patient himself can of course consent to being treated ignoring the wishes of his parents.

In practice, the reasons for judging a patient '*Gillick* aware' will need to be very carefully considered and fully recorded in the notes. For such a serious and complex matter as refusal of a life-saving blood transfusion a minor would probably require exceptional maturity to be '*Gillick* aware'. (see for example *Re E*, Chapter 3, page 29)

Minor under 16, not '*Gillick* aware'

(1) Parents cannot be contacted
Applying the doctrine of necessity, if parents cannot be contacted in time to give consent, a doctor is under a duty to do what is necessary to save life or preserve health.

(2) Neither parent consents
Any one person with parental responsibility may give valid consent to treatment on behalf of the child, even if all the others object. The difficulty arises when parents are contacted and neither will consent despite receiving a proper explanation of the serious risks of withholding blood.

Given sufficient time, the proper course is to seek the court's guidance. It is suggested that the consultant in charge telephone his defence union and the hospital manager. The latter will no doubt wish to instruct the hospital's solicitors to make an emergency application to the High Court for a specific issue order under s.8 of the Children Act 1989 or invoke the Court's inherent jurisdiction under s.100 of that Act. A duty High Court Judge is available at all times to hear such cases. It is highly desirable that the parents are also represented before the judge.

The attitude the judge will take can be predicted from two phrases of Lord Justice Taylor:

'. . . it is settled law that the court's prime and paramount consideration must be the best interests of the child'

'. . . the court's high respect for the sanctity of human life imposes a strong presumption in favour of taking all steps capable of preserving it save in exceptional circumstances.'

In that case, baby J was a ward of court born prematurely and with severe brain damage. Despite the second of the above principles, the Court of Appeal found the doctors justified in their decision not to ventilate him again.

(*Re J (a minor) (wardship: medical treatment)* [1990] 3 All ER 930, [1991] Fam 33 (CA))

Although the sincere beliefs of parents and children have been accorded great respect, in all the reported cases judges have dispensed with the need for parents' consent and permitted life-saving blood transfusions.

Extreme urgency

However rapidly solicitors, barristers, judges, and court officials respond, the emergency court procedure must inevitably take several hours. When the need for blood transfusion is so urgent that judicial help cannot be awaited, the doctor is faced with the decision to treat the patient on his own responsibility without consent. In making this decision he should consider:

(1) The existence of the doctrine of necessity;

(2) NHSME guidance 'A guide to consent for examination or treatment' (reproduced below);

(3) The consistent attitude of the courts, favouring the preservation of life in these cases;

(4) The social implications.

Example

A 20-year-old Jehovah's Witness is in the resuscitation room shocked and unconscious from a bleeding duodenal ulcer. Her

Refusal of parental consent to urgent or life-saving treatment.

Where time permits, court action may be taken so that consent may be obtained from a judge. Otherwise hospital authorities should rely on the clinical judgement of the doctors, normally the consultants, concerned after a full discussion between the doctor and the parents. In such a case the doctor should obtain a written supporting opinion from a medical colleague that the patient's life is in danger if the treatment is withheld and should discuss the need to treat with the parents or guardian in the presence of a witness. The doctor should record the discussion in the clinical notes and ask the witness to countersign the record. In these circumstances and where practicable the doctor may wish to consult his or her defence organization. If he/she has followed the procedure set out above and has then acted in the best interests of the patient and with due professional competence and according to their own professional conscience, they are unlikely to be criticized by a court or by their professional body.

(National Health Service Management Executive; HC(90)22 page 5)

father strongly objects to blood transfusion, saying this would also be his daughter's wish. He threatens to sue the hospital. Her mother disagrees and urges that blood be given.

Reference to Chapter 3 Fig. 3.1 guides us to classify her as 'adult: unconscious or of unsound mind' and leads to Fig. 3.3. She is unable to give or refuse consent. Nobody else, however emphatic, can consent or refuse on her behalf. We have next to consider whether she has previously expressed her refusal, free of undue influence and intending it to apply in this circumstance.

It is the authors' view that if there is doubt as to the validity or applicability of such an 'advance directive' it is proper for the doctor to disregard it. Applying the legal doctrine of necessity the doctor should then do, without consent, whatever is necessary in the short term to save her life.

Time is short in this situation. If possible a colleague should be involved, notes kept and witnessed, and relatives given a respectful hearing.

Suicidal patients

Key points

1. A competent adult, who is not 'sectioned' cannot be restrained nor forced to accept medical treatment against his will. To do so is assault and battery.
2. A competent adult is one who can understand the broad nature of the treatment being offered even though he may be insane and sectionable.
3. An insane person, having been 'sectioned' under s.2 or s.3 can be compulsorily admitted to hospital for assessment or psychiatric treatment. This also permits medical treatment against his will but only for the consequences of the suicide attempt.
4. A hospital owes a duty of care to prevent those at risk of suicide from harming themselves. Vigorous efforts should be made to persuade patients not to harm themselves until they agree or are sectioned.

Most people who harm themselves and are brought to an emergency department want treatment and consent to it. Some however refuse essential treatment, run away, or do themselves further harm. All are emotionally upset but few will be certifiably insane or 'sectionable'. Emergency department staff undoubtedly wish to protect them from physical harm as well as giving the right emotional support. The principal legal questions which arise in this situation are:

(1) What is the scope of the duty of care owed to those who harm or threaten to harm themselves?

(2) What power have staff to restrain patients and impose treatment on the unwilling?

The answer, as ever, is given by applying general law to particular circumstances, especially the law concerning consent (Chapter 10) and negligence (Chapter 11).

The duty of care owed to those at risk of self harm

Every patient that comes to an emergency department is entitled to be cared for. The staff must take reasonable care to

ensure their patient does not come to harm, either as a result
of failure to treat him or through other foreseeable hazards.

Police failed to inform a remand centre of a prisoner's
known suicidal tendencies; the centre did not take special
precautions; he hanged himself. The police were held
liable. Lord Justice Farquharson said: 'Counsel submits
that there can be no duty to safeguard a man from his
own act of self-destruction . . . The position must, in my
judgement, be different when one person is in the lawful
custody of another, whether that be voluntary, as is
usually the case in a hospital, or involuntarily, as when a
person is detained by police or by prison authorities. In
such circumstances there is a duty upon the person
having custody of another to take all reasonable steps to
avoid acts or omissions which he could reasonably foresee would be likely to harm the person for whom he is
responsible.'

(*Kirkham* v. *Chief Constable of the Greater Manchester
Police* [1990] 2 QB 283 (CA))

What is reasonable? What is foreseeable? It depends on
the facts of each case but the authors suggest it includes
(depending upon the apparent risk) regular or even continu-
ous observation and, if he threatens to abscond, vigorous

Hospital staff knew an in-patient was a serious suicide
risk. Two of the three nurses left the ward. When the third
attended to another patient he left the ward, jumped from
a roof, and was injured.

He successfully sued the hospital for failing to observe
him continuously. The court held the degree of care
required was proportionate (a) to the risk and (b) the
potential for harm to a particular patient.

Selfe v. *Ilford and District Hospital Management Committee* (1970) 114 SJ 935; *The Times* 26th November 1970)

efforts to warn the patient of the risks, to persuade him to stay and accept treatment, warning his relatives, his general practitioner, and the police if he in fact absconds. The duty probably includes avoiding local hazards such as unlocked high windows.

The legal duty of care does not require any illegal act, especially physical restraint to which consent would be required. That is assault and battery.

'Self-discharge' Forms

Some emergency departments try to persuade patients to sign a form stating they are leaving contrary to professional advice. Such a form is no more than evidence that such professional advice was given but ignored. The advice given should be recorded in the notes.

Attention-seeking behaviour

When it is certain that threats or actions do not constitute a genuine suicide risk it may be considered excessive to engage in vigorous persuasion and involve the police, family doctor, and others if he leaves. In this situation it is recommended that this should be a considered and positive decision, recorded in the notes together with reasons.

The power to impose treatment against a patient's will

Are there circumstances in which treating a patient without consent does not amount to assault and battery? In this context it is important to remember the distinction between medical treatment and psychiatric detention and treatment. Almost invariably the emergency department treatment of self harm is medical treatment and the same rules apply as for any other medical treatment unless he has been 'sectioned' under s.2 or s.3 of the Mental Health Act. The formal detention of a mentally ill patient for psychiatric assessment or treatment is a separate issue (see page 56 and Chapter 15).

Adult of sound mind
This means a person over 18 capable of understanding the broad nature of the treatment offered. This legal test does not

require them to be 'informed' nor understand the implications. Such patients cannot lawfully be forced to accept any physical treatment.

It must surely be good practice to endeavour to persuade them of their folly and it might be considered negligent not to do so.

Adults 'sectioned'

If an adult is capable of understanding the broad nature of his treatment yet refuses, he cannot be treated. However once an application is completed under sections 2 or 3 (only) of the Mental Health Act 1983 he can be treated without consent for the physical consequences of his suicide attempt. (*B* v. *Croydon Health Authority* [1995] 2 WLR 294; see Chapter 15).

Adults of unsound mind

Where a patient is unconscious or otherwise incapable of understanding the broad nature of what is being offered, the doctrine of necessity may be invoked and careful and proper restraint and treatment may be given for his physical condition (*Re F*, Chapter 10). For example the patient may be so drunk or drugged he is unable to understand what is offered. Good medical practice requires us to discuss this with carers and relatives if there is time and it is practicable but there is no requirement first to obtain anybody else's consent.

Previously expressed intentions: advance directives or 'living wills'

During the above discussion with carers it may emerge that an unconscious patient had previously, while of sound mind, made it clear he did not want to be treated in this situation. Normally these wishes should be respected but cases of self harm may be an exception. With the Suicide Act of 1961, suicide ceased to be a crime but it did not become a lawful act. Aiding and abetting suicide remains a criminal offence. There have been recent manslaughter convictions of doctors for 'gross negligence' and police prosecution of professional people is no longer rare. In this atmosphere it is possible that those caring for a suicide patient who deliberately let him die could be charged with the offence of aiding and abetting suicide (Suicide Act 1961 s.2(1)).

Is there any legal power to restrain a patient?

If a patient is capable of broadly understanding the nature of treatment offered he is 'of sound mind' even though 'sectionably insane'.

From a series of cases in the eighteenth and nineteenth centuries it appears that citizens have the power to restrain a 'dangerous lunatic' from doing mischief (see Chapter 15). The Code of Practice under the Mental Health Act refers to this in guarded language, implying that it is limited to cases of sectionable insanity and where the person will go on to be sectioned. The limits of this power have not been tested in the courts and great caution is advised.

In any event it should only be used in extreme cases where a patient is undoubtedly seriously mentally ill and is dangerous and an approved social worker and two psychiatrists can all be relied upon to agree with this diagnosis.

Children

1. If a young person is 'Gillick competent' which means being sufficiently mature to understand the implications of their decision (not the same as the adult's test of mental capacity) then they can consent to treatment as adults can. However the courts may find this test requires very great maturity where life-saving treatment is refused, as in the case of an adolescent Jehovah's Witness (see page 27).

2. Minors over 16 can consent to treatment as adults can. Their ability to refuse treatment if a parent consents is legally controversial (see Chapter 10). The High Court can declare their treatment lawful if there is time. Also there is no minimum age for a 'section' under the Mental Health Act.

3. Children who are not 'Gillick competent' may be treated with consent given by one person who has parental responsibility. If one cannot be found the doctrine of necessity may be invoked and life-saving or health-saving treatment given. In the unlikely event that parents are available yet refuse necessary treatment an urgent application to the High Court should be made if there is time. Otherwise the senior doctor must decide whether to treat without consent. Remarks applying to the children of Jehovah's Witnesses (page 38) can be applied to this situation. It is

even less likely a doctor will be criticized for saving a life since the dilemma here arises from folly rather than the sincere religious beliefs of Jehovah's Witnesses.

Example

A 30-year-old man is brought to hospital by his parents for treatment shortly after taking a large paracetamol overdose and alcohol. He is sleepy but rouseable. He understands he may die if not treated. He refuses any investigation or treatment. The duty psychiatrist is called to see him and confirms he is not mentally ill and will not be 'sectioned'.

He is a competent adult. His irrational refusal must be respected. Proper efforts should be made (and witnessed) to persuade him to accept admission and treatment and prevent him harming himself further.

Violence in the department

Key points

1. Violent attacks are usually punishable crimes.
2. Anyone may arrest a person who deliberately strikes and injures another.
3. In general only physical illness excuses criminal responsibility for violent attacks. The influence of drink or drugs is no excuse in most crimes. Mild or moderate mental disorder is no excuse.
4. **Never** hit back.
5. Always call the police.

Emergency department staff 'smile and whistle under all difficulties', tolerantly shrugging off violent assaults and threats. They endure rudeness with tolerant restraint and are sympathetic to high spirits and the physical disinhibition of the distressed. However it is no part of a doctor's, nurse's, or porter's duty to take physical injury in the course of their work. Emergency departments will become more difficult to man unless vigorous measures are taken to prevent such incidents. Reporting every attack on emergency department staff to the police is justified. Staff who witness incidents should keep notes for use in court.

First the categories of violent behaviour which are recognized as crimes and the penalties they attract from a court are outlined. We then consider the rights and powers of self help which can be exercised on the spot and which exist and arise from those crimes.

Some violent acts recognized as crimes

Common assault

The crime
Intentionally or recklessly making someone fear immediate and unlawful personal violence. Examples include threatening words, placing the hand on a weapon, or shaking a fist in someone's face.

The punishment
See battery.

Battery

The crime
Intentionally or recklessly inflicting unlawful personal violence on someone. The slightest touching without excuse or
consent can amount to battery and it does not need to be rude
or aggressive.

The punishment
The maximum penalties for either common assault or battery
are six months' imprisonment or a fine. A likely punishment
is a community penalty.[1]

Assault occasioning actual bodily harm
(Offences Against the Person Act 1861, section 47)

The crime
Intentional or reckless assault or battery on someone which
actually results in any hurt or injury. Actual bodily harm can
be mere bruising or psychiatric harm.

The punishment
The maximum penalty is five years' imprisonment. In more
serious cases tried in the Crown Court (e.g. use of dangerous
weapon; more than minor injury by kicking or head butting
etc; serious violence on those working in contact with the
public) a prison sentence is likely.

In less serious cases tried by magistrates the maximum is six
months' imprisonment or a fine or both. A likely punishment
is a community penalty.[1]

Wounding or inflicting grievous bodily harm
(Offences Against the Person Act 1861, section 20)

The crime
Recklessly or intentionally wounding (breaking the continuity
of the skin) or doing grievous bodily harm (really serious
injury). In order to commit this offence the offender must at
the time realize he runs the risk of doing harm.

Examples of sufficient harm have been: 'glassing'; punching
and breaking a facial bone; striking the scalp with a blunt
weapon causing a wound requiring four stitches.

The punishment
The maximum penalty in the Crown Court is five years' imprisonment. In less serious cases brought before the magistrates the maximum is six months' imprisonment or a fine or both. Prison is likely.[1]

Wounding or causing grievous bodily harm with intent
(Offences Against the Person Act 1861, section 18)

The crime
Wounding or causing grievous bodily harm either **intending** to cause grievous bodily harm or **intending** to resist lawful apprehension. It differs from the above (s.20) offence in that the prosecution must prove he either intended really serious harm or he intended resisting apprehension and doing some sort of harm. Examples have been: 'glassing'; kicking a man on the ground in the head; stabbing; throwing corrosive fluid.

The punishment
It is triable only before the Crown Court and carries a maximum penalty of life imprisonment. Expect between three and eight years in prison.

These are the main offences arising from violence to the person short of murder, attempted murder, and manslaughter. Violent acts can attract other criminal charges including causing criminal damage and offences under the Public Order Act 1986 such as affray and fear and provocation of violence.

Damage to property: Criminal damage
(Criminal Damage Act 1971)

The crime
Damaging another's property intending damage or reckless as to whether it is damaged.

The punishment
Although the maximum penalty is ten years, most offenders are punished by a fine and compensation order.

The more serious offence of aggravated criminal damage is committed where the offender also either intends or is reckless as to endanger the life of another. It is easy to imagine such an event in an emergency department with sick patients and attached equipment. This attracts a maximum of life imprisonment.

Lawful physical self help

(Rights and powers arising from unlawful activity of others)

Arrest

Arrestable offences
In general all offences carrying a penalty of five years or more are arrestable. All the violent crimes listed above are arrestable except for common assault and battery in which no injury results.

Anyone may arrest the actual offender, caught in the act or later. If the offence has already been committed **anyone** may arrest a person he has reasonable grounds to suspect.

How to arrest:

(i)   inform the offender clearly that he is arrested and what for, even if this is obvious.

(ii) Restraint may be applied but only if necessary to prevent escape.

(iii) Police should be called immediately and the prisoner handed over to their custody.

(iv) A careful record must be kept of all these events including times and who was present.

Proceedings against the offender may be discontinued at any time by the police or the Crown Prosecution Service especially if there is not a reasonable prospect of a conviction. It is important therefore to keep good, contemporaneous notes and be willing to attend court.

The arrest must be based on the exercise of a legal power or the arrested person can sue for false imprisonment.

Preventing breach of the peace
A breach of the peace is a violent disturbance where harm is done or likely to be done to a person or, in his presence, to his property. It does not have to amount to a criminal offence.

Anyone can take reasonable steps to prevent a breach which is taking place or merely threatened in his presence. 'Those reasonable steps in appropriate cases will include detaining him against his will short of arresting him'.[2] Any citizen has the power to arrest:

(a) where a breach of the peace is committed in their presence or

(b) he believes, on reasonable grounds,
   (i) that such a breach will be committed in the immediate future

   or

   (ii) a breach has occurred and the arrestor believes, on reasonable grounds, that a renewal is threatened.[3]

Restraining a dangerous mentally disordered person
Where a person is sectionably insane and dangerous the common law allows him to be restrained (see next section and Chapter 15). This does not amount to arrest and is only appropriate where it is intended to admit him for his mental disorder.

Self defence
It is proper to use reasonable force

• to defend oneself

• or another person

• or in preventing a crime

What is reasonable force depends on the nature of the threat or the crime but in general like must match like. For example it would not be reasonable to use a knife to defend oneself from a fist. This principle of law is important to staff since it provides a defence should a criminal charge or civil claim arise from their actions. Never hit back or do what could be misinterpreted as hitting back. It is a criminal offence and a serious professional error.

Other considerations

Relevance of duty of confidentiality
Staff have an ethical obligation not to divulge anything they have learnt in the course of their practice. Reporting a violent incident to the police can be done without giving any confidential clinical information. The two types of disclosure must not be confused. A patient who is violent may himself speak of his clinical condition or the reason for his attendance but that is up to him. There is no ethical reason not to report such a crime.

Violence by the mentally disordered
Mental disorder is very seldom so severe as itself to amount to an answer to a criminal charge. It would have to be proved that the person was so ill he did not know what he was doing

or did not know it was wrong. If insanity is proved it does not result in an acquittal but enables the court to deal with him in a variety of ways including ordering treatment for his disorder, in or out of an institution.

Something falling short of legal insanity, such as depression, may make it harder for the prosecution to prove the necessary mental element of an offence.

Violent drunks or those intoxicated by drugs
The courts take a poor view of acts of violence done under the influence of drink or drugs which offenders have taken to deprive themselves of their self control or their knowledge of what they are doing. For most criminal charges, not only is self-induced intoxication no defence but, if the offender claims he did not mean to do it because he was intoxicated, the prosecution are absolved from proving any mental element and need simply prove the act was done. It is thus easier to obtain a conviction.

There is an exception in certain crimes of 'specific intent' where intoxication is a defence if it is so severe as to make the offender incapable of forming the necessary intent. Wounding or causing grievous bodily harm with intent is the only crime of this class among those listed in this chapter. Even if the accused succeeds in this defence, he can still be convicted of a lesser but similar offence.

Violence by the physically ill
If a person commits an act of violence while not in any voluntary control of his physical actions due to some external factor he is not guilty of any offence because he is legally in a state of automatism. Examples of such external factors are: insulin induced hypoglycaemia, cerebral concussion, and drugs taken under medical supervision (see Chapter 15, page 60).

Patients who have been battered
Emergency department staff will have experience of comfort and support and will have local information of a practical nature, such as the location of women's refuges.

The victim can use the law in two ways:

1. To punish the assailant
He should contact the police immediately. They may wish to make a forensic examination and thought should be given

before physical evidence is destroyed. The emergency department doctor is often later asked for a report and so should make detailed notes.

2. To prevent further incidents
An application to a civil court for an injunction may be necessary. This is a judicial command and disobedience is punishable as contempt of court. It may be useful in some domestic skirmishes where the criminal law punishment may not be suitable. The victim should contact a local solicitor, law centre, or citizens' advice bureau. This may also need a medical report from the emergency department doctor.

Examples

1. A clinically depressed man has been waiting for the psychiatrist when he runs about the department, threatening patients and staff, and breaking equipment.

On the face of it he has committed the crimes of common assault and criminal damage. It is proper to arrest or restrain him as he is committing a breach of the peace. It is also proper to use appropriate force to prevent a crime. It may be better, especially if the patients are not at risk, for hospital staff to call police to do this.

If he remains violent the psychiatrist should consider 'sectioning' him under s.2 of the Mental Health Act so that he can be sedated.

The fact that he is clinically depressed may make it difficult to prove the necessary mental element of his crimes if he is prosecuted.

2. A drunk man is brought to the emergency department with minor injuries. He has been struck in the face but is able to walk about and answer questions. He is abusive and he strikes a nurse who is treating him, bruising her.

Anyone can arrest him though it is sensible to call the police to do this. Witnesses should immediately make notes. His drunkenness will not excuse him at his trial.

End notes

1. Magistrates' Association guidelines 1993
2. words of Lord Diplock in *Albert* v. *Lavin* [1982] AC 546
3. *R* v. *Howell* 73 Cr App R 31 (CA)

Mentally ill patients

Key points

1. Compulsory admission should not be undertaken lightly but an alternative solution sought first.

2. 'Sectioning' is usually under s.2 and permits treatment for the psychiatric problem and its physical consequences.

3. Section 2 admission requires an approved social worker and two doctors, one of whom must be approved, the other should know the patient.

4. The custody of patients brought by police under s.136 should remain the responsibility of the police.

4. The Mental Health Act gives no power to treat patients who are not 'sectioned'. Outside the Act there is power, in limited circumstances, to restrain and give minimal treatment.

6. Emergency department staff can be held responsible if a dangerous patient causes harm to others in the department or if he escapes.

This part is principally concerned with power to compel those who require admission for mental disorder but will not accept it. It does not apply to any physical illness.

The quality of care of a mentally disordered patient will inevitably depend on the experience, sensitivity, and the reservoir of good humour of the emergency department staff.

Most mentally ill patients who come to the emergency department are uncomplicated to diagnose and manage. They may be followed and treated by their family doctor or the psychiatric out-patient department. Only a few will be troubled enough to require admission and most accept informal admission. It goes without saying that every effort should be made to pacify, reassure, and strive for cooperation, voluntary admission, and treatment. Other texts describe techniques for this, avoiding confrontation and conflict. Although compulsory admission can be necessary it is often harmful to self-esteem, reputation, relationships with family, social workers, psychiatrists, and other doctors. When all other efforts have failed the compulsory powers may be required.

'Sectioning': compulsory admission under the Mental Health Act 1983

Under section 2

This is the section for the emergency department. It will require the attendance of an approved social worker (ASW) or nearest relative and two doctors. One doctor must be 'approved' by the Secretary of State and the other should if possible know the patient or, if he does not, he should also be 'approved'. The social worker's job is to make the application after interviewing the patient and if satisfied that this is the best way to treat him. Both doctors must examine the patient and feel able to support the application on the grounds that:

'he is suffering from mental disorder of a nature or degree which warrants the detention. . .'

And

'he ought to be so detained in the interests of his own health or safety or with a view to the protection of other persons' (but not on account only of drug or alcohol dependence or sexual immorality or deviance).

If the patient does not go on to be admitted either compulsorily or informally the ASW and doctors are expected to make arrangements for his further care (page 3, Code of Practice under the Mental Health Act).

Effect

Once the form is completed he may be detained in hospital for 28 days and treated without consent for his psychiatric illness and its physical consequences. This includes being able to sedate him, treat an overdose or self-inflicted wounds.

Under section 3

Whereas section 2 is for admission for assessment section three enables detention for a longer period for treatment. It may be appropriate for known psychiatric patients. In any case the procedure is very similar and a section 2 admission can later be converted into a section 3 admission. Both sections permit treatment.

Not under section 4
Under this 'emergency' section an approved social worker (or the nearest relative) may make the application and one doctor, who ought to know the patient and does not have to be approved, can provide the medical recommendation. The effect of this is the patient can be detained against his will for 72 hours but the section does not enable any treatment without consent. Furthermore, unless a psychiatrist is involved, there will be no hospital bed. This section is of little practical value to an emergency department.

Patients brought by police: section 136
The police may arrest a mentally disordered person in a public place and bring him to a place of safety including an NHS hospital. That person may be detained there for 72 hours to enable him to be interviewed by an ASW and doctor and arrangements made for his care. If he escapes the person having his custody can retake him.

Emergency department staff have no obligation to accept custody of an arrested patient but if they do accept custody they may be liable for the consequences of his escape and for breaches of the requirements of the Police and Criminal Evidence Act (including record of time of arrival; informing another person; facilitating access to legal advice when requested). If they do not wish to accept custody they must make it clear to the police that this aspect remains police responsibility. Section 136 does not enable treatment without consent. Until he is 'sectioned' under section 2 or 3 a patient cannot be sedated without consent (unless he lacks capacity to consent, see below).

Powers over patients not 'sectioned'

Except under formal 'section' or arrest under section 136(6), the Mental Health Act does not give any legal power over a patient. Only in the circumstances described below, the minimum necessary restraint and treatment is permitted under the existing common law so that the patient will not be able to bring an action for assault.

A practical consideration
If a patient is sedated before being interviewed or examined by the ASW and the recommending doctors, it will be difficult

for them to make a proper assessment. There is a risk that they may decline to make any recommendation.

No capacity to consent: doctrine of necessity
If an adult is unconscious or so severely mentally disabled that he is unable to understand in broad terms the nature of treatment being offered, the doctrine of necessity may be invoked. This enables the minimum necessary treatment to be given to save life or prevent deterioration in health without consent. Treatment must be in accordance with accepted psychiatric practice and strictly in the interests of the patient. In the case of a child, reasonable efforts should first be made to obtain the consent of one person with parental responsibility.

'Severely disturbed and dangerous'
Review of a series of eighteenth and nineteenth century cases suggests that any person has the power to restrain a 'dangerous lunatic' from doing harm. This principle has not been affirmed this century although the Code of Practice under the Mental Health Act suggests that some think it does still exist. If it does exist it applies only to someone who is actually 'sectionably insane' at the time. In modern language 'a patient suffering from a mental disorder which is leading to behaviour that is an immediate serious danger to himself or others may be given such treatment as represents the minimum necessary response to avert that danger' (page 58, Mental Health Act Code of Practice; see Chapter 15).

It may be lawful to restrain or sedate a dangerous patient who is definitely about to be sectioned. Remember, however, that sedation may cause the social worker and psychiatrists to be 'unable to assess' the patient. Besides this, there is no legal power to hold a patient in an emergency department while awaiting psychiatric assessment.

A breach of the peace
Anyone may take reasonable steps to prevent a breach of the peace (a violent disturbance) if it is committed or reasonably appears to be about to be committed in their presence. This includes physically detaining the person but not, of course, sedating him.

The duty of care

The emergency department staff will naturally be under a duty to take reasonable care of a mentally ill patient and, short of an illegal act, do what is reasonably necessary to prevent him harming himself. This duty extends to protect others which almost certainly includes other visitors to the emergency department and anybody outside if a dangerous patient absconds and does harm.

L, 'a defective', had many convictions for violence and had been sentenced to be detained in a mental hospital at His Majesty's pleasure. He was let out on licence and beat a woman up with a piece of wood. She sued the hospital. The jury was directed that the doctors and hospital would be liable to the woman if the doctors had not exercised reasonable care. The jury so found.

(*Holgate* v. *Lancashire Mental Hospitals Board* [1937] 4 All ER 19)

A prisoner, attacked by H, a mental defective when both their cells were left open, failed to win damages. Although the court found the prison had a duty to take reasonable care of a prisoner, there was no reason for it to have considered H more dangerous than an ordinary prisoner.

(*Ellis* v. *Home Office* [1953] 2 All ER 149)

Seven borstal boys working on Brownsea Island under the control of three borstal officers, cast off the motor yacht 'Silver Mist' which was damaged. Its owner sued the officers' employer. The House of Lords upheld the award of damages finding that the officers owed the yacht's owners a duty of care to prevent the boys doing damage, if there was a manifest risk. In letting them escape they had failed in that duty.

(*Dorset Yacht Co* v. *Home Office* [1970] AC 1004)

Children

There is no minimum age for compulsory admission under the Mental Health Act. However there are several alternative provisions for children and the paediatric team should first be consulted.

Examples

1. Police bring a large, aggressive, and disturbed man to an emergency department. They say that they have arrested him under section 136 of the Mental Health Act and have brought him to a place of safety. They wait patiently for the arrival of the approved social worker and psychiatrists but, before these arrive, announce that their shifts are ending and they are leaving the man in the care of the emergency department.

It is important not to accept custody of the man. There is no power to sedate him until he is 'sectioned' under section 2 or 3, except possibly under the ancient 'common law' power whose existence is ill defined and uncertain and which certainly does not apply if he is not actually insane at the time. This may be perceived as a minefield of trouble.

The correct action is to insist he remains in the custody of the police who can then remain with him or remove him.

2. An unkept man comes to the emergency department complaining the government is slandering him by means of loudspeakers. The duty psychiatrist is asked to see him but the patient walks out before he arrives.

The department has a duty to care for him but its staff can only do what is lawful. This means attempts can be made to persuade him to stay, to contact his family, his doctor, or the police. There is no power to restrain him.

Patients under guard

Key points

1. A prisoner or person in police custody has the same right to confidentiality and to give or withhold consent as any other patient.
2. Insist on making a full and proper assessment.
3. It is unwise to accept requests to perform forensic assessments without having received training.
4. Never agree to accept custody of anyone.

It is rather common to see people in custody brought to emergency departments. They may be prison inmates accompanied by prison officers or people under arrest in the company of policemen. Usually such attendances cause no difficulty. Emergency department staff will think it right to help the policemen who on another occasion may save them from violence. Some concessions may be proper such as accelerating the patient through the department. It is vital, however, that the doctors' and nurses' professional integrity is never compromised.

The fact that someone is a detained prisoner does not affect his right to be treated nor does it affect his right to consent to or refuse treatment nor his right to confidentiality.

Consent

Any consent must be freely given. Care must be taken where the giving of consent could affect the prisoner's situation or prospects. In this circumstance it is wise to have the consent witnessed.

> A prisoner unsuccessfully claimed the prison doctor had injected him with drugs against his will, not as treatment but as part of his custody. Mr Justice McCowan remarked '. . . where, in a prison setting, a doctor has the power to influence a prisoner's situation and prospects a court must be alive to the risk that what may appear, on the face of it, to be a real consent is not in fact so.'
> (*Freeman* v. *Home Office* [1983] 3 All ER 589)

In other respects the law is the same for prisoners as for other patients. In particular, a competent adult, prisoner or not, may refuse any treatment, however irrational or harmful the consequences of the refusal.

This point was emphasized in a case in which the Home Secretary sought guidance over his duty or power to force feed a hunger striker. Mr Justice Thorpe reversed the old decision of 1909 that it had been the duty of prison officials to preserve the health of prisoners in their custody and that duty extended to force feeding. Mr Justice Thorpe said 'The right of the defendant to determine his future is plain. That right is not diminished by his status as a detained prisoner.'

(*Secretary of State for the Home Department* v. *Robb* [1995] 2 WLR 722;
Leigh v. *Gladstone* [1909] 26 TLR 139)

Confidentiality

The patient is entitled to the same confidentiality as any other. It is proper to communicate details to his captors only if he freely consents to this.

Inadequate assessment or treatment

The emergency department staff may feel under pressure to assist the custodians in their duty. For example, it may be suggested that the prisoner was brought only for a particular condition or injury to be excluded. It may be suggested, that he is inventing his condition to avoid facing something he would rather not. Under such circumstances emergency department staff must be particularly careful to take a full history and examine properly. There may be more to a case than initially meets the eye. The only safe course is to insist on making as full an assessment as any other patient would receive. If a patient requires admission or any other treatment it must be offered irrespective of other considerations. If this is obstructed it must be witnessed, documented and if necessary, reported.

Forensic Examination

Emergency department staff may be asked by police or prison staff to offer an opinion as to the cause or nature of an illness or injury. This is the task of the clinical forensic medicine specialist or police surgeon. Any opinion expressed will be acted on and may be tested in court. It should only be given after careful reflection. Forensic examination requires special training, particularly in cases of rape.

Inability to take a proper history

There may be circumstances where a proper history cannot be taken due to the embarrassing presence of the guard. It must be made clear and recorded in writing that the patient has not been properly assessed. The emergency department staff must however discharge their duty of care to their patient. It may be appropriate to insist the guards organize themselves so that proper conditions for the consultation exist in the emergency department or else ensure the prison doctor or police surgeon sees him.

Interrogation in the department

The code of practice under the Police and Criminal Evidence Act 1984 provides (at paragraph C 14.2): 'If a person is in police detention at a hospital he may not be questioned without the agreement of a responsible doctor'. This means the doctor at the moment caring for the patient, not his chief.

This ensures that any doctor has priority over the police in access to a patient. Breaches of the code can be the subject of a formal complaint.

Custody

Never accept any custody of a prisoner or a mental patient brought to a place of safety. It is incompatible with the therapeutic role of medical and nursing staff. Should the prisoner escape, staff may be liable for damages.

Example

Police bring a drunk handcuffed patient with facial injuries saying they 'want his face assessed'. They will not permit him to be seen alone and a proper history and examination cannot be carried out.

This is wholly unsatisfactory and will eventually lead to disaster even if not on this occasion.

It is essential to insist politely that a proper assessment must be made if the patient will allow it. If they refuse this it must be documented and senior help obtained in the form of the hospital manager or a consultant. They should obtain a satisfactory outcome or the way is clear for a complaint to the Police Complaints Authority.

Motorists

Key points

1. The police are entitled to be given the identity of a driver involved in most types of motoring offence.
2. A patient whose condition may impair his driving must be warned and the warning recorded.
3. Where the police require from a patient a specimen of breath, blood, or urine the doctor must be informed and may object to any or all of these on the ground that it would be prejudicial to the proper care and treatment of the patient.
4. Forensic specimens should normally be taken by an external doctor, usually a police surgeon.
5. Diagnostic specimens cannot be used by police without consent.

A well-worn expression says 'the motor car makes criminals of us all' and emergency department staff may, depending on their experience, come to adopt either a draconian or a protective attitude to drivers. Balance can be coupled with professional detachment. The security of mind which stems from knowledge of the law makes this felicitous state easier to achieve.

The principal circumstances where emergency department staff may require knowledge of their legal position involving motorists are:

(1) police enquiry as to the identity of a driver;
(2) unfit persons who may drive and cause danger;
(3) drivers suspected of having excess alcohol.

It is worth considering the importance of public confidence in the profession and that the principal function of the emergency department is saving life and health.

Police enquiry as to identity of driver

In general the police are not entitled to any information about a patient unless he consents to its being given. A rare exception to this rule is in section 172 of the Road Traffic Act 1988. It requires disclosure to the police of information leading to the identification of a driver of a vehicle involved in a traffic offence. Failure to do so is itself a criminal offence.

A general practitioner treated a man and a girl who said she had been injured in a road accident. Nineteen days later a constable requested the doctor to disclose the identities of the two patients who he suspected, had been in a car that had been stolen and driven dangerously. The doctor refused. He was prosecuted and fined £5 for failing to comply with the predecessor of section 172. He appealed and lost. It was held, even a doctor carrying out his professional duty came within the section.

(*Hunter* v. *Mann* [1974] QB 767)

Patients with conditions which may make driving dangerous

The duty of care
Doctors owe a legal duty of care to those members of the public whom they should foresee are likely to be harmed by their acts or omissions. It is essential to warn anyone whose driving may be impaired and to record this warning in the notes. If a doctor fails to give and record such a warning he may himself be held liable for all the damage in a resulting accident. In particular this should be considered where there is:
- an eye injury, eye patch, or drug affecting vision;
- a drug affecting consciousness or concentration, for example general anaesthetics, opiates, or blood pressure lowering drugs;
- alcohol;
- a condition which may affect consciousness or concentration such as epilepsy, psychiatric illness, poor control of blood sugar, transient cerebral ischaemia, disorder of heart rhythm;
- any factor which may affect movements of the limbs including dressings, slings, or splints.

Information to DVLA

Holders of driving licences are obliged to inform the Driver and Vehicle Licensing Centre as soon as they are aware of any condition which may affect safe driving, other than simple disabilities not expected to last more than three months. The obligation to inform does not arise until the driver is personally aware of the condition. It is therefore necessary a doctor should always warn a patient of hazards to driving.

A doctor is not legally obliged to warn anyone other than his patient. However if concerned that a patient may not heed advice and therefore be a source of danger it is open to him to inform the Licensing Centre himself. It is obviously good practice first to warn the patient of this intention which he must be prepared to explain and justify.

The GMC advises that disclosure may be made 'in confidence' to the medical adviser at DVLA if a doctor is unable to persuade a patient to stop driving. The patient must be informed of the disclosure.

(Duties of a Doctor: Confidentiality. GMC, October 1995)

Dangerous unconcern

It is surely right to inform the police when exceptionally obdurate individuals ignore all warnings and knowingly drive off in a dangerously unfit condition. They should be warned they will be reported.

Drivers and excess alcohol: Statutory basis

The Road Traffic Act 1988 is a modernized version of the 1967 Road Safety Act which introduced the breathalyser. Section 5 creates offences of driving or being in charge of a motor vehicle with alcohol concentration in breath, blood, or urine above the prescribed limits.

Stage 1. Screening and arrest

The Act enables a constable in uniform to administer a screening breath test if he suspects a driver has alcohol in his body. If the driver fails or refuses the test he can normally be arrested. But he cannot be arrested if he is a patient in hospital.

Stage 2. Definitive specimen for analysis

Whether or not there has been Stage 1, a constable can require a suspected driver to provide a specimen for analysis. If he is in hospital this must be blood or urine. The constable decides which of these it shall be unless a doctor says it cannot be blood. The driver commits an offence if he fails without reasonable excuse to provide the specimen. He also commits an offence if he provides a specimen and it contains 80 mg or more of alcohol in 100 ml of blood or 107 mg alcohol in 100 ml of urine.

Special position of hospital patients

Before the constable can 'make the requirement' of breath for Stage 1 or of blood or urine for Stage 2, he must notify the doctor in immediate charge of the patient. If the doctor then objects the constable cannot 'make the requirement' and that is the end of it. The doctor may only object if it 'would be prejudicial to the proper care and treatment of the patient':

1. to require the specimen or
2. to give the patient the obligatory warning that he will be prosecuted if he refuses to provide the specimen.

Providing a blood specimen

The Act says 'A person provides a specimen of blood if and only if he consents to its being taken by a medical practitioner and it is so taken'. If he does not himself specifically consent to its being taken for this purpose, taking blood for that purpose will amount to assault and battery. If he does not consent he will be treated as refusing to provide the specimen required. (He clearly cannot reasonably provide or consent to a specimen if he is unconscious but want of comprehension due to drunkenness is not an excuse)

Who should take the blood specimen?

To satisfy the Road Traffic Act requirements any medical practitioner, not necessarily a police surgeon, may do so. If the police are not able to coax their police surgeon out of his bed they may be tempted to ask emergency department staff for help. Very careful consideration should be given before agreeing to this because:

(1) it is an activity which is not therapeutic and which may damage the reputation of the profession and the hospital;
(2) there is no obligation to do it;

(3) without specific training, errors will occur, for example in tube labelling, specimen division or alcohol skin swab contamination. This can cause embarrassment in court and in theory could render the doctor liable in negligence. Don't do it!

Blood taken for diagnostic purposes
This cannot be used for Road Traffic Act analysis unless the patient agrees.

By the Police and Criminal Evidence Act 1994 s.11.(1) 'human tissue or tissue fluid which has been taken for the purposes of diagnosis or medical treatment and which a person holds in confidence' is excluded material.
Police can only obtain access to this by application to a circuit judge and he can only allow such access in the very limited circumstances described in Chapter 12.

Example

A car driver is unconscious after a traffic accident and smells strongly of drink. Police ask the doctor if this patient can be approached for a specimen of blood or urine. When told he is unconscious they ask the doctor to take a specimen of blood for them since his driving has resulted in the death of a child.

Since the patient is unconscious he cannot consent to anything. No one can consent for him. Taking a specimen of blood without consent amounts to assault and battery. On the other hand, doing so for therapeutic purposes is not battery since it is for the purpose of saving life or preventing deterioration in health and is lawful under the doctrine of necessity if in the patient's best interests.

The following day the officers ask for the cross-match sample which was taken on arrival. They may not have this either without the patient's consent.

5 Officialdom

- **Enquiries about patients 70**
- **Illegal drugs 79**
- **Police access to patients 75**

Enquiries about patients

Key points

1. All clinical information is confidential and, without consent, may not be disclosed except in defined circumstances.

2. The police do not have access to clinical records nor even to times of arrival and discharge.

3. The identity of a driver must usually be disclosed on enquiry by police.

4. A suspected terrorist must be reported to police.

5. While child protection agencies must receive medical and nursing cooperation, the disclosure to them of clinical information is a professional responsibility and cannot be automatic.

Enquiries from patients' relatives and friends as to their well-being seldom present difficulty. A patient will usually give his consent but, if he cannot, and it is in his best interests, it is fairly easily implied. On the other hand, when officials make enquiries the culture of helpfulness may predominate with the risk of improper disclosure.

The fact that a practice is widespread or of long standing does not make it lawful. Enquirers may assert that revealing confidential information must be done because it is 'in the public interest'. This is seldom true and must be weighed critically. What is undoubtedly in the public interest is maintaining the confidential relationship between doctor and patient.

Medical confidentiality begins from the position that everything is secret and there are important exceptions to this rule, either imposed by law or permitted by the ethical guidance of the GMC. In every case of doubt as to whether details should be disclosed, the process of reasoning should follow the same order. In general, the law treats medical secrets with respect.

Enquiries by the police

Requiring the identity of a driver

It is an offence for anybody to fail to disclose, when asked, information which may lead to the identification of a driver who is alleged to be guilty of a motoring offence.

Concerning terrorism

It is an offence to fail to report any information which may lead to the apprehension of a terrorist or prevention of terrorism connected with Northern Ireland.

All other circumstances

The law does not entitle the police to any other information about any patient. Without his consent, they may not learn any medical details, nor of any injuries nor the time of his arrival or departure, nor even if he attended at all. This means that attendance registers and department computer screens are confidential and must not be shown to the police. It is incumbent on the department's senior medical staff to ensure this confidentiality is preserved (see Chapter 12).

Disclosure in the public interest
The GMC advises that cases arise where disclosure in the public interest may be necessary such as when someone may otherwise be exposed to death or serious harm. This gives ethical permission to a doctor to reveal details without consent. It does not put the doctor under a legal duty to do so.

A woman had been murdered near a mental hospital by repeated stabbing. The police sought to know the comings and goings of the in-patients and sought to see the hospital's returns to the Department of Social Security for National Insurance purposes of patient admissions and discharges. The consultant psychiatrist refused their request.

The police applied to Cardiff Crown Court where a circuit judge decided that the returns were not 'excluded material' for the purposes of the Police and Criminal Evidence Act (PACE) and ordered the consultant psychiatrist to give police access to the returns.

The consultant appealed to the Divisional Court (Lord Justice Evans and Mr Justice Morland) which found that the returns were indeed excluded material and the circuit judge had been wrong.

Mr Justice Morland said: 'The words (of PACE) must be given their ordinary and natural meaning . . . even if the result might impede a police investigation into a terrible murder and allow a very dangerous man to remain at large and a real risk to others. . .

Parliament defined excluded material as a matter of public policy, presumably because it considered that the confidentiality of records of identifiable individuals relating to their health should have paramountcy over the prevention and investigation of serious crime . . .

Often records of admission and discharge from a hospital or clinic would reveal the aspect of health for which a person was a patient, for example a mental or maternity hospital, venereal disease clinic, or accident and emergency department.'

(R v. *Cardiff Crown Court, ex parte Kellam* (1993) The Times, 3rd May)

Enquiries by employers

Clinical information should not be disclosed without consent. It may be wise to obtain this in writing since claims for damages may arise out of incidents at work. However H.M.

inspectors of factories carrying out their duties to investigate, for example accidents in the workplace or ill-health caused by industrial processes have a legal right: 'to require any person whom he has reasonable cause to believe to be able to give any information relevant to any examination or investigation . . . to answer . . . such questions as the inspector thinks fit to ask and to sign a declaration of the truth of his answers'. This extends to clinical information. It is an offence to fail to comply with the inspector's requirement; the maximum fine is £5000.

Enquiries by nursing homes or other institutions

Due to their mental or physical state, some patients are not able to give or withhold consent to the disclosure of information. In cases where it is in the patient's interests to share information with carers, this may be done without consent provided it is made clear the information is confidential.

There may be other requests, such as for a report on an accident form, which may not necessarily be in the patient's interests. If consent is not forthcoming or is not possible, due to incapacity, no report or other details can be given.

Enquiries by child protection agencies

A professional approach
An outline of the proper action to take when child abuse is suspected is described in *Accidents and Emergencies in Children* by Morton and Phillips in this series, and a doctor or nurse may then have little difficulty squaring their professional conscience. 'You may release information without the patient's consent but only if you consider that the patient is unable to give consent, and that the disclosure is in the patient's best medical interests.' (para 11, Duties of a Doctor; Confidentiality. GMC October 1995). But it is somewhat less clear how properly to answer enquiries by interested parties when a train of suspicion begins elsewhere.

In any event, the decision to disclose information should be reached from the same perspective as in other cases; that all clinical information is confidential unless one of the exceptions obtains where information may be disclosed or unless a person with parental responsibility consents to disclosure.

There is no legal right vested in any social worker or other official to obtain clinical information. A doctor must exercise his discretion and only disclose it in the best medical interests of the patient.

Social services
The nature of enquiries by social services varies between authorities and between individuals. Usually they are measured and professional. Sadly, in one author's experience, this is not universal. When an emergency department doctor judges it appropriate to report circumstances to the social services he will do so and an enquiry may be a helpful prompt to do this. Nevertheless, the responsibility for the decision remains that of the doctor. When in doubt it is essential to take several minutes to consider and, if necessary, first consult a senior paediatrician, the consultant in charge of the department, or a defence union. As a practical consideration it is in the interests of children to maintain good and trusted channels of communication. It may be appropriate in many cases to share information with the community paediatrician rather than with a stranger on the end of a telephone.

'At-risk' registers and auto notification
The methods of detecting and preventing physical or sexual harm to children are far from perfect. A part of the machinery of child protection is the detection of frequent attendances at different emergency departments on the ground that inadequate parents may vary their places of attendance to allay suspicion.

In some departments there is a practice of notifying every attendance by any child to a central body, usually a social services department. These bodies may distribute to emergency departments and other places lists of children considered at risk. Emergency department staff may be encouraged to scan these lists for the name of every child that attends and report attendances of children on the list.

This may be acceptable as being in the best interests of children at risk but it is difficult to justify the practice of routine disclosure in the face of the carefully worded description of the permitted circumstances of disclosure in the GMC's guidance. (paras 10, 11, Duties of a Doctor; Confidentiality. GMC October 1995)

Police access to patients

Key points

1. No one may enter a department without implied or express permission, either of which can be withdrawn. A constable however has specific but limited legal powers of entry.
2. No one may remove or examine any notes, no one may examine any computer record showing confidential material.
3. Do not mislead a constable nor help anyone to avoid detection or arrest.
4. Ensure that any disagreement with police is witnessed and contemporaneous notes kept.

The presence of the police in an emergency department may be reassuring yet raise doubts in the minds of patients as to the professional detachment of the staff. Good relations with the police is valuable but it is important to know the boundaries of good conduct they must respect. Emergency department staff must have control of the physical space of their department to provide proper care and to maintain proper professional relationships with the patients.

The necessity of this may not be understood by an inexperienced police officer. Therefore emergency department staff may wonder:

- when police have a right to enter;
- when they can be excluded from a department or part of it; and
- what measures exist to enforce and maintain the rules of the game.

When police have the right to enter

Constables have extensive powers of entry to prevent crime and to make arrests:

(1) to arrest someone for an arrestable offence or with an arrest warrant (he must have reasonable grounds for suspecting the person is there);
(2) to recapture an escaped prisoner or mental patient (he

must have reasonable grounds for suspecting the person is there);

(3) to save life or limb;

(4) to prevent serious damage to property;

(5) to deal with or prevent a breach of the peace (usually a fight or scuffle).

The police can pursue other aspects of their duty once they are in the department (such as arresting for arrestable offences, searching people in it for controlled drugs, weapons, and stolen goods, and seizing such items). They cease to be able to do so once they are told to leave unless still exercising one of the specific powers of entry.

Obstruction
It is an offence to obstruct a constable in the execution of his duty. This can include disposing of evidence or warning or assisting a suspect to escape. It does not include properly preventing a constable entering if he does not have one of the above powers of entry.

When police can be excluded from a department

Effect of instruction to leave
The emergency department is on land belonging to the hospital's 'trust' board who have the right of exclusive possession. The person in charge of the department for the time being is the agent of the hospital. Through him, the hospital can exclude anyone and once he, as its agent, has told someone to leave they become a trespasser, unless they have a specific legal power of entry. This applies to the police or anyone else.

Notes and computerized records
By the Police and Criminal Evidence Act 1984 (PACE) these are 'excluded material'. The police have no right to seize nor to look at emergency department notes, hospital notes nor computerized records on paper or on screens. The material is confidential and protected by the Act.

Questioning by police of detained patients in the emergency department
This may not be done without permission. (PACE Code of Practice C14(2): 'If a person is in police detention at a hospital

he may not be questioned without the agreement of a responsible doctor').

Enforcing the rules

Polite firmness must be the correct approach with a professional and detached attitude. It is essential not to deceive the officer or help a suspect to escape, but every patient is entitled to proper care and treatment. An enthusiastic officer could be tempted to threaten a member of the department with arrest and criminal prosecution. It is proper to insist that such a threat is repeated in the presence of a professional colleague and the conversation recorded in writing. A telephone enquiry to a defence organization will generate reliable advice.

It has to be recognized as a practical necessity that the principal means of keeping anyone out of the clinical areas is their sense of good behaviour and the power of the police themselves. Hospital security staff may be naturally cautious over confronting the police. In law the only means of excluding someone from property is by civil action for trespass. This may prove a meagre deterrent.

Allowing bad behaviour by police officers to go unreported is harmful in the long term both to the police force and to the maintenance of social order.

Remedies for breaking the rules

Civil action in the courts
A trespasser can be sued for nominal damages for the fact of his trespass and substantial damages for the consequences of it. In most circumstances this will be an academic remedy although evidence that is heard by a court of outrageous behaviour will receive judicial comment which may lead to disciplinary action. However a telephone call to the hospital manager for confirmation of the officer's instruction to leave may impress him with the seriousness of the matter.

Complaint to the Police Complaints Authority
A complaint of unacceptably bad behaviour by a police officer may result in disciplinary action. The Police Complaints Authority considers not only complaints of illegal acts and abuse of authority but also conduct likely to bring discredit on the reputation of the force.

Appropriate matters for complaint
Complaints should not be made lightly or for minor breaches.
The Police Complaints Authority has far-reaching powers over
every policeman and can damage his career or worse. In any
case an investigation by the Authority is a miserable business
for its subject. An ill-considered complaint will also impover-
ish any good relationship between a department and its local
police station.

Illegal drugs

Key points

1. Think carefully before removing a package from a conscious patient. The law does not require it.
2. Having taken possession of a controlled drug, other than one lawfully prescribed, it must be destroyed or given to a constable.
3. Destroying drugs can in some circumstances amount to obstruction of the police.
4. In all contact with illicit drugs, be witnessed and keep witnessed notes.
5. Only specifically licensed doctors can prescribe diamorphine, dipipanone, or cocaine to addicts for their dependence.

Drug abuse is increasing and those involved come frequently to emergency departments. They may be unfortunate dupes or cynical dealers. Severe penalties are attracted by those convicted of trafficking and police may show interest in these patients. Emergency department staff will receive patients who have drugs on them. Take care to avoid innocently committing an offence against the Misuse of Drugs Act 1971 since the prosecuting authorities have lately turned their sights onto the professions.

Most of the situations described have not been tested in the courts and the judges interpret the Misuse of Drugs Act somewhat inconsistently. It is unsafe to rely on common sense and the certainty of good intentions being understood. To be the defendant in a criminal trial is expensive: in money, emotion, and time. Even to be prosecuted and acquitted because you have a good defence is no fun at all. Never risk it.

Drug Offences

The Misuse of Drugs Act makes it an offence to possess, supply, or possess with intent to supply any controlled drug listed in schedules 1, 2, and 3 of the regulations made under that Act. Doctors and the sister in charge of a department are privileged in that they do not commit an offence by possessing and supplying the controlled drugs listed in schedules 2 and 3 (see Chapter 14).

However if they possess or supply schedule 1 drugs, such as cannabis, lysergide, mescaline, psilocin, or raw opium, they commit offences against the Act. Furthermore supplying any illegal substance, including any schedule 2 or 3 drugs that have not been prescribed, to someone will make them accessories to his crime of unlawful possession which he commits on receiving them.

Giving the drugs back
By whatever means emergency department staff come by illicit drugs they must never therefore give them to a patient or visitor. Returning someone's own drugs to him amounts in law to the crime of supplying. The only acceptable fate of illegal drugs which come into the possession of emergency department staff is that they be destroyed or surrendered to the police.

The unconscious patient with a suspicious package

It is difficult not to take possession of it in removing and storing his clothes. Once this has happened it cannot be returned to the patient unless it is undoubtedly lawfully prescribed.

It obviously cannot be known what the substance is. If it is a schedule 1 drug the staff commit an offence by merely possessing it unless they either destroy it or give it to a policeman as soon as possible.

'It is the duty of the custodian not to hand them back but to destroy them or to deliver them to a police officer so that they may be destroyed'.

(*Lord Keith in R* v. *Maginnis* [1987] AC 303)

Police not in pursuit
There is no requirement to report a crime (except in connection with Northern Ireland terrorism) and under these circumstances it may usually be right to destroy the drugs.

Police interested
It would be different if the patient were being pursued by police who indicated their suspicion that he may have drugs

on him. To destroy the drug then may be destroying evidence and would amount to obstructing a constable in the execution of his duty or even an act tending and intended to pervert the course of public justice. The drug should be handed to the police immediately. The law does not require staff to give any words of explanation or other information to the police and it will usually be a breach of professional confidence to do so. However when the matter comes to court a judge can insist on answers to his questions.

For this and other reasons it is essential that every action involving the package is witnessed; that clear, contemporaneous notes are kept and countersigned by those witnesses.

The conscious patient with a suspicious package

Don't touch it.

A patient with a lawfully prescribed drug

If a patient has a controlled drug on him which he is entitled to possess, such as a registered addict with prescribed methadone, a doctor or the sister in charge may take possession of it, keep it for the patient and return it or administer it to him. It must be kept under the same secure conditions as other schedule 2 controlled drugs (in the 'DDA' cupboard) and a proper record kept.

The addict who has 'lost' his lawfully prescribed drugs

Only a medical practitioner with a Home Office licence may prescribe for an addict diamorphine, dipipanone, or cocaine except for relief of pain due to injury or organic disease. There is nothing in law to prevent a doctor prescribing anything else but irresponsible prescribing will result in a restriction being placed on the doctor's ability to prescribe controlled drugs. There is no obligation to prescribe for addicts and to do so without careful consideration may result in unwelcome popularity.

Before treating this particular suffering it may be advisable to take precautions against 'double scripting' by contacting the patient's own doctor or his dependency unit doctor, or the staff of the Chief Medical Officer at the Home Office on 0171 273 2213.

CHAPTER 6

Local difficulties

• **Difficulty in referral 82** • **Insufficient resources 83**

Key points

1. Referral of patients to a more senior doctor discharges an inexperienced doctor's duty of care.
2. Referrals must always be properly recorded.
3. A hospital's management may now be sued, as well as its doctors, if it fails to provide a safe system of care.

Difficulty in referral

The service of an emergency department can only be as good as its hospital will allow. Overtired or over-confident junior members of in-patient teams may be tempted to take advantage of the inexperience of a casualty officer. He may be dissuaded from making a formal referral against his better judgement or the reluctant response may be unacceptably slow. In these circumstances patients come to harm and in the ensuing enquiry the blame is usually placed fairly and squarely on the shoulders of the casualty officer. This problem may arise:

(1) where the casualty officer is unable to make a decision having recognized the insufficiency of his knowledge and experience, or

(2) where he has identified the need for admission but it has not occurred.

In either case he discharges his duty of care by referring to a senior for advice or help. This is because in doing so he does all he can to make the patient safe.

The importance of proper and accurate documentation cannot be emphasized too strongly. this must include:

(1) the name and post of the doctor to whom the patient is referred,

(2) the time of referral,

(3) a summary of the facts communicated in the referral.

This should be routine and not confined to referrals to 'rogue elephants'.

The above steps will save the emergency department doctor from being unfairly sued. The patient's interest is paramount and courts will not look favourably on evidence of internal squabbles or poor communication where there has been a bad outcome. The practical method of making the patient safe is immediately to discuss the difficulty with the emergency department consultant who can then make the referral to the consultant of the receiving team.

Insufficient resources

This is not a suitable topic for lengthy discussion in a pocket book but is touched on as a developing area of law relevant to emergency services which will influence their development.

Legal challenges of funding decisions
Several attempts have been made to challenge in the courts the funding decisions of various NHS bodies. In every case the judges have refused to enter this arena saying it is not the

---

Four people on a sluggish orthopaedic waiting list unsuccessfully sued the Health Secretary for breach of his statutory duty to provide a comprehensive health service. Lord Denning said 'the Secretary of State says he is doing the best he can with the financial resources available to him: and I do not think he can be faulted in the matter.'

(R v. *Secretary of State of Social Services ex parte Hincks* (1980) unreported (CA))

court's role to usurp the function of the N.H.S. body by making its decisions for it. The only circumstances in which it would intervene would be where the decision was unreasonable to the point of irrationality, or where it was illegal or procedurally irregular.

The judges have unswervingly held on to this principle in a series of cases.

A father applied to the court for an order that Cambridge District Health Authority must fund private treatment for a young girl with leukaemia. This was to take the form of a third course of chemotherapy and a second bone marrow transplant. Her doctors had advised the authority that further treatment was not in her best interests and it had accepted that advice. The Court of Appeal rejected the father's application.

Sir Thomas Bingham, the Master of the Rolls said: 'The courts are not, contrary to what is sometimes believed, arbiters as to the merits of cases of this kind. Were we to express opinions as to the likelihood of success of medical treatment, or as to the merits of medical judgement, then we should be straying from the sphere which under our constitution is accorded to us. We have one function only, which is to rule upon the lawfulness of decisions.

Sir Stephen Brown said: '. . . I am unable to say that the authority in this case acted in a way that exceeded its powers *or which was unreasonable in the legal sense'*.

(R v. *Cambridge District HA, Ex parte B* [1995] 1 WLR 898)

Insufficient funds causing unsafe system

The situation is different where inadequate funding has resulted in harm to a patient. As well as a 'trust' or health authority being vicariously liable for the negligent acts of its doctors and other employees it now also has 'primary' liability if it provides an unsafe system of care. This means the hospital itself is under a duty to provide a patient with a reasonable standard of care. This implies that an emergency department must function according to the standard reasonably to be expected of such a unit. This is new law and may become a powerful implement in the improvement of emergency departments.

Mrs Bull claimed her son had been injured at birth by asphyxia because a doctor was not available to attend her as the service was on two sites and the system for calling the registrar had broken down. Lord Justice Slade accepted that the authority owed her a duty of care and said `The duty of a hospital is to provide a woman admitted in labour with a reasonable standard of skilled obstetric and paediatric care, in order to ensure as far as reasonably practicable the safe delivery of the baby or babies and the health of the mother and offspring thereafter.'

(*Bull* v. *Devon AHA* [1993] 4 Med LR 117 (CA))

This important case marks the early development of a new focus of liability. If this principle is followed in other cases it will gives us a legal means of twisting our employers' tail. They will come to realize that to avoid liability they must provide a proper and safe unit or else close it down.

CHAPTER 7

Writing reports

• **Criminal cases 87** • **Practical points 90**

Key points

1. The doctor's duty of confidentiality applies to written statements
2. Most reports are factual. Adding an opinion makes the writer an expert who is liable to be cross-examined as such.
3. Experts should only express honestly held opinions and not take sides.
4. Never exaggerate your own expertise.
5. Keep notes of consultations.

Criminal proceedings are the commonest occasion for a medico-legal report in the form of a factual description of injuries, requested by the police. Victims, their solicitors, and others may approach doctors for reports to aid civil claims for compensation. These too are usually essentially factual, but the opinion of the doctor may also be required making the report an 'expert' report. The distinction is blurred since some expertise is always necessary anyway to elicit and interpret the facts.

A court receives two kinds of evidence. **Factual** evidence is what a witness has actually perceived and any witness can give it. **Opinion** evidence is only given by an expert to assist the court to interpret facts. An expert can also, obviously, give factual evidence. Junior doctors should be most wary of being asked for their opinion in this context. Consultants are usually considered experts within their own field.

Criminal cases

Purpose

Medical reports are needed:

(1) to assist the prosecution in formulating charges;

(2) as part of evidence for the committal (first stage) proceedings before the trial;

(3) at trial either:

    (a) the basis for agreement between prosecution and defence as to type and extent of injuries; or

    (b) a script for the judge and lawyers when the writer gives evidence in court.

Content

It should describe the injury or other harm. It may help to indicate severity by reference to the treatment required. The report is a document for the court and not a medical note and so, in criminal cases, the history is usually irrelevant. If included it will be erased by the prosecution as hearsay. A useful form of words which could be used is: 'I was asked to see Mr Smith and as a result of what he told me I examined him and found the following: . . . ' It is helpful to give precise and factual descriptions of the injuries with measurements and references to anatomical features. Diagrams should be reduced to words since they cannot be typed into the statement although they or any other form of picture could be included and referred to as an exhibit. Make it clear what was directly observed by the writer, and what has been learnt from others, as for example by reading the notes.

Opinion

It is vital the writer does not stray outside his expertise. Opinions of aetiology, pathology, or cause of injury carelessly tossed in will be pounced on by both prosecution and defence. The writer will be compelled in the witness box to display his knowledge. Witnesses are not obliged to give opinions and junior doctors should be very certain of them before doing so.

Civil cases

The form of a report will depend on the solicitor's instructions. He may request a report restricted to the facts. He may also require an opinion concerning prognosis, outcome, or perhaps aetiology. In addition an opinion of the care given by others is sometimes requested.

Purpose

(1) To provide the solicitor with the facts for his case.

(2) To be the basis of settlement of the case at any stage.

(3) To be part of the pleadings (documents exchanged before trial defining the issues in the case).

(4) For the information of judge and lawyers at the trial to indicate what the doctor is likely to say in the witness box.

(5) To limit what may be said in the witness box.

Content: all civil reports

There should be a statement of the reason for the report, the sources on which it is based and the qualifications and experience of the writer. A history should be included based on the patient's history and other information such as hospital notes. There should be a record of the relevant physical findings on examination and an interpretation of any investigations. A final summary is useful and the report must be signed and dated.

Opinion

Expert reports
It is important to give a clear indication of the degree of expertise of the writer including experience, training, and qualifications. As well as setting out the factual findings give an opinion founded upon them. This will usually be a prognosis of the injury and the degree of suffering and disability the victim has had and will have. In awarding damages for personal injury, courts are less concerned with past pain and suffering than quantifiable losses such as loss of earning ability, loss of enjoyment of life, and need for nursing or other help.

Medical negligence cases
As well as eliciting and setting out factual findings and giving an opinion of them the writer will consider the patient's treatment. He will be expected to indicate what in his opinion was a proper standard of care and whether the patient actually received care of that standard. The solicitor's instructions should make plain what

---

Mr Justice Cresswell set out the main duties and responsibilities of expert witnesses in civil cases:

1. Expert evidence presented to the court should be and should be seen to be the independent product of the expert, uninfluenced as to form or content by the exigencies of litigation.

2. An expert witness should provide independent assistance to the court by way of objective unbiased opinion in relation to matters within his expertise. An expert witness in the High Court should never assume the role of an advocate.

3. An expert witness should state the facts or assumption upon which his opinion is based. He should not omit to consider material facts which could detract from his concluded opinion.

4. An expert witness should make it clear when a particular question or issue falls outside his expertise.

5. If an expert's opinion is not properly researched because he considers that insufficient data is available, then this must be stated with an indication that the opinion is no more than a provisional one. In cases where an expert witness who has prepared a report could not assert that the report contained the truth, the whole truth and nothing but the truth without some qualification, that qualification should be stated in the report.

6. If after exchange of reports an expert witness changes his view on a material matter having read the other side's expert's report or for any other reason, such change of view should be communicated (through legal representatives) to the other side without delay and when appropriate, to the Court.

(*The Ikarian Reefer* [1993] 2 Lloyd's Rep at p 81)

---

is required but in all cases of professional negligence the standard to indicate is that of an ordinary competent practitioner in that field and not necessarily the writer's own higher standard.

Practical points

Style

Reports are to help medical laymen interpret facts. They should be couched in simple direct language with anatomical and pathological terms explained. Circumlocution is better than obscurity. When in doubt, facts and opinions should be included rather than left out. Reports are always served on the other party to the litigation to inform him of the issues and prevent him being taken by surprise at the trial. Most civil cases are settled at an early stage but any of them could go on to trial. In that event the report will receive very close scrutiny and will be the 'script' for the evidence the writer gives in the witness box, on which he will be cross-examined.

Bias

Objectivity and detachment are expected of a professional witness even though he is paid for his evidence. He is expected

---

In 1976 seven people were convicted of possession of explosives and received up to fourteen years imprisonment. The principal evidence against them had been nitroglycerine under fingernails and on gloves, identified by thin layer chromatography. It was implicit in the finding of guilt that there was no innocent explanation for this.

The scientific expert witnesses called by the Crown had failed to disclose to prosecuting counsel certain negative tests on the fingernail material. This information was not therefore revealed to the defence or the court.

Their appeal against conviction was allowed. The failure of disclosure had been a material irregularity in the trial.

(*R* v. *Maguire and others* [1992] 2 All ER 433)

to assist the court rather than take sides. Only genuinely held opinions should be expressed and the writer has a duty to provide a straightforward, not a misleading opinion. He must not mislead by omitting material factors which go against his opinion. Incentives to favour one party may exist in the prospect of further instructions and there is a risk of acquiring a reputation of being one of the 'guns for hire'. At present there is regrettably little sanction against the misleading expert, other than that of reputation, except in the most blatant and outrageous cases.

In criminal cases, failure by a prosecution expert to disclose material which may have some bearing on the case will be grounds for appeal against conviction.

Conclusions

All the facts on which an opinion is grounded must be capable of proof in court by evidence. The writer must also be able to justify his opinion. It may be based on direct experience but need not necessarily be. It can also stem from academic knowledge, training, and interpretation of the work of others. It is not necessary or proper to argue the patient's case for him in the report; this can be done as well or better by the lawyers. The purpose of the report and of the doctor's evidence is to help the court come to a conclusion. Avoid expressing an opinion on the ultimate issue of fact before the court by writing, for example, that one party is 'to blame' or 'negligent'.

Communication with solicitor

It is important to understand what the solicitor requires from a particular medical report. Any reservations about one's own expertise or suitability should be made known straight away. Solicitors vary in experience and may be unfamiliar with the structure of the medical profession and may assume emergency physicians have extensive knowledge of specialist surgery. Openness in this area will enhance and not harm a reputation. If a solicitor requests an examination too soon after an accident for a proper prognosis it must be explained that any report will be provisional. When in doubt consider use of the telephone, for example if it is suspected a patient is malingering or if an expensive investigation is felt necessary or if the solicitor appears to have blundered in some way. The report itself and associated letters will become court documents.

Fees

Solicitors are obliged to pay a reasonable fee for a medical report (unless an unreasonable one is previously agreed!). What is reasonable depends mainly on time spent on the report and the normal reward of a doctor of that seniority and experience. It is worth keeping a diary of actual time spent. The BMA gives some guidance over fees. Payment is the solicitor's personal responsibility unless, exceptionally, when instructions are given he says otherwise. Fees are due immediately unless he has previously identified the case as having Legal Aid in which case a reasonable fee is paid after the solicitor is reimbursed. Even here payment should be within about a month. Regrettably a minority of solicitors do not pay and the amount may be too small to be worth suing for. If such firms request further reports it may be sensible to insist on payment before releasing them. As payment is a professional obligation, a complaint to the Solicitors' Complaints Bureau might help.

Litigants in Person

If a litigant in person requests a report it must be explained in advance this is not a National Health Service activity and it attracts a fee. Litigants in person are usually less detached in their approach. They may not understand the doctor's duty to be impartial and it may be difficult to write a report they will find satisfactory. There is no obligation to undertake this type of work. Junior doctors should seek consultant advice before doing it.

Notes

Retain any notes of the consultation. They will be the only direct record of it and may be needed in court. Furthermore if a dissatisfied litigant attempted to sue the maker of the report the notes would constitute the bulk of his evidence in his own defence.

Consent

Never release a report without the written consent of the subject. Beware of unauthorized attempts by others to view it.

CHAPTER 8

Going to court

• Compelling attendance: summonses and orders 93

Key points

1. Take the patient's notes.
2. Stay neutral.
3. Make sure you are properly paid.
4. Expect your time to be wasted.

The prospect of court may be a source of apprehension. The remedy is adequate preparation. A doctor is likely to attend court:

(1) as a witness of fact in a criminal case;

(2) as a witness of fact in the Coroner's Court;

(3) as an expert witness in civil proceedings;

(4) as a witness of fact in civil proceedings.

The important considerations are: when attendance is compulsory and what fees are payable and when. It is also worth considering what is expected in the witness box.

Compelling attendance: summonses and orders

A reluctant witness is an antagonistic witness and lawyers pause before coercing a doctor into court. They are easily persuaded that doctors are busy and that unnecessary absence from their work will cause suffering to others. The opportunity should always be taken to make clear the notice required of any hearing date. Dates should be selected for the doctor's convenience as far as possible. This is more likely to be achieved in civil proceedings than in criminal proceedings.

Legal proceedings, particularly criminal cases, involve an army of officials, the least sparkling apparently being delegated to contact witnesses. The legal process has one overriding priority, from the lawyer's perspective, which is not to upset the judge. Judges become irritated if the progress of a case is frustrated by absence of witnesses due to the case going faster than the lawyers anticipated. Lawyers therefore summon more witnesses than can be heard in one day, just to be on the safe side. This is exacerbated by the court listing system since court officials (over whom the parties to the case have no influence) will list more cases than can be tried by the court because a proportion of cases can be expected either to 'crack' with a late plea of guilty being entered where a trial was otherwise expected, or settle, because the parties in civil proceedings have come to an agreement at the last moment.

A very few enlightened court staff arrange for doctors to be at work on an hour's standby to give evidence. Usually, with tiresome regularity, emergency department doctors receive unnecessary instructions to attend court and are sent away on arrival or are kept waiting for most of a day before being informed they will not be required until the next day. The only compensation lies in the fees which may be claimed for wasted time. There is no reason not to make the process expensive for those who waste a doctor's time.

We explain the effect of summonses and similar documents.

In criminal cases

In the Magistrates' Court
Anything other than an actual summons is simply a polite invitation to attend. A magistrate or his clerk can issue a summons if satisfied a witness can give material evidence and will not attend voluntarily. A magistrate can also issue a warrant to arrest a witness if he is satisfied:

(a) a summons will not secure his attendance, or

(b) • he was served with the summons and paid a reasonable sum for expenses **and**

• he has no excuse for failure to attend **and**

• he can give material evidence or produce a material document or thing.[1]

Refusal to give evidence or produce a document or thing renders the witness at risk of a month in prison and a fine up to £2500. It must be proved that he had notice of the date of the trial. Witnesses are required to suffer considerable disruption of their business and private lives.

In the Crown Court
Proceedings are in two parts, the second being the trial itself. The first or committal stage is in the magistrates' court and is usually a formality in which witnesses' written statements are acknowledged and the witnesses are made the subject of witness orders. Witness orders can be full or conditional. A full order obliges the witness to attend at the trial. A conditional witness order means the witness's statement is likely to be read out in court. Attendance is not required unless he is given notice requiring him to attend. That notice converts it into a full witness order. The Crown Court also can issue a witness summons any time.

Failure to obey a full witness order, a conditional witness order with notice to attend, or a witness summons 'without just excuse' is contempt of court and renders the witness liable to be arrested, brought before the court, made to give his evidence and punished by up to three months imprisonment.[1]

In civil cases

Civil trials are in the High Court or the County Court depending on the size of the claim. Disobeying orders of the High Court, including orders to attend, is likely to cause greater pain in view of the draconian powers of High Court Judges. The High Court can issue a subpoena *ad testificandum* (requiring attendance to give evidence) or *duces tecum* (requiring attendance to give evidence and bring documents). Disobedience is contempt of court even if not deliberate. Simply forgetting the date is enough. A High Court Judge has the power to punish contempt by an unlimited fine and imprisonment up to two years.

The County Court can also issue witness summonses either *ad testificandum* or *duces tecum*. Failure to attend is contempt, punishable by a fine.

In coroners inquests

Unlike all other proceedings in the courts of England and Wales which are adversarial, there are no 'parties' before a Coroner's Court (no prosecution and defence, no plaintiff and defendant). Proceedings are by inquisition where the Coroner decides what evidence he requires, directs his officers to undertake investigations, determines which witnesses to summon and he is the primary interrogator of those witnesses. Other interested parties (such as the family of the deceased, the driver of a motor car) may question witnesses at the Coroner's discretion.

Although a Coroner has a discretion to hear witnesses he has not himself called, it is rare for him to do so and the party wishing to call the witness has no means of compelling attendance. Therefore a doctor required to give evidence before an inquest can only be compelled by the Coroner himself. Usually witnesses for an inquest are only requested informally to attend. The Coroner can issue a witness summons if he considers a witness may not attend voluntarily. His summonses can only compel attendance of witnesses and not the production of documents. A Coroner can only summons a witness in his own district. To compel attendance of a witness outside his district, or the production of documents, he must arrange for the High Court to issue a subpoena, disobedience of which is punishable as above. Disobedience of the Coroner's witness summons is punishable by a fine of up to £1000.

Setting aside witness summonses

Occasionally a witness is summoned but is convinced that he can give no useful evidence at all. Perhaps the wrong person has been chosen or the evidence he could give could not be relevant to the issues in the trial. All courts which can compel attendance of witnesses also have the power to excuse those witnesses from attending.

The issue of a witness summons or subpoena is a purely administrative act. If a defendant in criminal proceedings or a party to a civil action chooses merely to fill in the relevant form naming the proposed witness, the court officials must issue the summons or subpoena. No consideration is given at this stage (other than in the Magistrates' Court or by a Coroner, see above) as to whether the witness could in fact give any useful evidence.

Consequently, if a witness is convinced that he can add nothing and may have been wrongly selected, application may be made to the court to set aside the summons or subpoena. This is a formal legal step requiring a hearing before a judge and legal advice would be desirable.

Fees

In any legal proceedings a witness's remuneration will depend on his status.

Witness of fact

Whatever his status or profession, a person who sees an incident such as a road accident or a fight will only be able to give evidence which is strictly factual. The rules of evidence do not permit him to express an opinion.

Expert witness

Where there are issues in the case requiring specialist knowledge or experience for their resolution, a person with that knowledge or experience may give his opinion to help the court interpret facts. Expert witnesses are called and paid for their opinions.

Professional witness

This is a hybrid who needs professional skill to explain factual matters encountered at work. As far as the law of evidence is concerned he is an expert. As far as fees are concerned he has a more lowly status and is not paid to have opinions as such. No witness is obliged to express any opinion and a professional witness may wish to discuss his status before doing so. Any accident and emergency doctor called to give evidence of a clinical encounter will always be at least a professional witness.

In criminal cases

Witnesses are entitled to be paid fees and expenses from central funds according to a scale drawn up by the Lord Chancellor.[2] Fees are payable if the witness attends at court whether or not he is called to give evidence. A doctor should ensure either the solicitor who called him or the court office provides him with the appropriate forms before leaving.

In civil cases

Fees should be agreed in advance between the doctor and the solicitor calling him except in clearly identified Legal Aid cases where they are on a scale. The solicitor is personally liable for the fees as soon as they are incurred. The British Medical Association's suggested scales can be a guide to negotiation.[2]

In coroners inquests

Fees for Coroners' work are regulated by statute. Doctors acting as professional witnesses, whether in preparing reports or attending to supplement such reports, or to give evidence of professional matters, will be paid according to a schedule set annually by the Home Secretary. However if an expert witness is engaged, by the Coroner or by an interested party, his fees are a matter for negotiation as in civil cases.

Giving evidence

Demeanour

It is essential to appear and to be impartial; unconcerned with the outcome of the trial. A professional person is above such feelings and should give a truthful and balanced account of his observations. Noticeable leaning towards one or other party will diminish his credibility and paradoxically lessen his value to the party calling him. He is not there for the police or the defendant but for the court. Answers should be simple and direct. It is not recommended to fence verbally with counsel who are in their own environment and will win. Use of humour is hazardous; a witness inadvertently repeating a common joke is as tiresome for the judge as it is for a doctor when patients do it.

Cross-examination

Evidence is first given 'in chief' in answer to questions by the barrister who called the witness. This is then tested by the opposing barrister by cross-examination. It is that barrister's professional duty to do his best to render uncertain some or all of the evidence against his client and he should do so with all the guile and subtlety at his disposal. He may seek to question the facts the witness has recounted and especially the accuracy of his memory or his notes. He may also question the credibility of the witness. In the case of a medical witness this will usually be limited to an attack on any opinions the doctor may have expressed, either in his statement or in the witness box. It is vital to confine expressions of opinion within the limits of a doctor's knowledge and experience.

A good cross-examiner will lay ambushes, using flattery and other devices to lure the witness out of the security of his limited knowledge before closing the trap by asking how he comes to know so much. It is safer, when a non-expert is asked for an opinion, to state a lack of sufficient expertise. It is then open to the parties to engage an expert and pay an expert witness fee.

Never get cross. A witness who feels he has been led to give a misleading or incomplete answer should make it known to the judge before leaving the witness box. Use the same form of address as counsel have already used (usually 'My lord', 'your honour' or 'Sir').

The duty of confidentiality

The General Medical Council requires that secrets learned by a doctor from a patient must not be disclosed without consent save under certain specific circumstances. One is when a judge orders it. Nevertheless it is both expected and proper to indicate that it is a breach of professional confidence and to invite the judge to reconsider or limit his insistence.

Getting to court

Check the court's documents for the correct time and place. In case of doubt a telephone call should be made to the court office before 4 p.m. (Civil Service!). On arrival, waste no time before meeting the solicitor or his clerk. If they have changed their mind, as usual, about calling the doctor he should insist his proper fees are determined before leaving the building.

What to take

The most important item is the case notes as well as any X-rays, photographs, electrocardiograms, or other instrument traces. The originals should be taken if available. The judge, lawyers, and jury may wish to inspect them. An expert should take any authorities on which he relies. A common problem occurs when prosecuting authorities fail to give the patient's name but instead give that of the defendant in the case. When this happens the doctor should take with him a record of the letters and telephone calls made attempting to discover the identity of the patient. The blame for an expensive and frustrating adjournment must be placed correctly. Although it usually will not matter since the lawyers so often decide at court that they do not need the doctor's evidence after all! Take a book or other distraction to occupy the long wait.

What not to take

Any umbrella, camera, coat, or thing of value. Cameras and tape-recorders are not allowed into the court; photography, tape recording, or drawing in court is an act of contempt. If you have a mobile phone switch it off.

End notes

1. s.3 Criminal Procedure (Attendance of Witnesses) Act 1965.
2. The present scale of fees is also published by, and obtainable from, the British Medical Association (Fees supplement 33 and its appendices).

Part 2

Reference section

The system

Medicine is practised within the infinitely complex machine
of human society. It is subject to many influences including
the super-vision by professional bodies as well as the activity
of government and its agents such as hospital management,
social workers, and police forces. The most potent influence is
the law.

History

Development of Common Law

In the beginning there was nothing. Anything was allowed
and the correction of wrongs was by whatever force was available to the victim. With the development of our civilization
came remedies administered by the King's courts which for
the sake of predictability tended to follow the principles of
their previous decisions and so evolved the Common Law.

Statutes

As the power of the Crown declined and that of Parliament
supervened Parliament became able to change the Common
Law by Statute (Act of Parliament or legislation). The struc-
ture of legal thought is founded on these events in history.
Modern judges are bound by the ancient principles of the
Common Law as modified by Statutes interpreted by them. It

is in this area that the Common Law particularly continues to grow, since Statutes are always imperfectly drafted without prescience of many of the circumstances the statute will bear upon. The extent to which Parliament may be under the thumb of the Crown, nowadays the Civil Service, influences the quality and content of statutes but not their interpretation. Most of England's and Great Britain's colonies were administered under English Law and on becoming independent states acquired the Common Law, current at the time of independence, and subsequently modified by their judges and their legislature.

The structure

Our courts have three types of jurisdiction. The casualty officer will encounter all three.

Criminal jurisdiction

Criminal jurisdiction considers prosecutions brought by one party against another where the principal aim is punishment. The purpose is to discourage. The prosecutor is almost always the Crown, or rarely, a private individual. It has to be proved that the accused person committed an offence. The standard of proof is higher than in civil courts; the jury or magistrates making the decision are meant to be 'sure' before convicting and proof of the facts constituting the offence must be 'beyond reasonable doubt'. The punishment or sentence is generally in the discretion of the judge or magistrates but they must follow guidance from superior courts. At the end of a criminal trial the first decision is 'Has the prosecution proved that the accused committed the offence?' if the answer is 'Yes' the second decision is 'What'll we give him.' The most serious offences are tried by the Crown Court in the form of a judge and jury. Lesser but often important offences are tried by a bench of experienced magistrates who are laymen advised on the law by a clerk who is often legally qualified. Magistrates' Courts were quite rightly called Police Courts until 1952.

Civil jurisdiction

Civil jurisdiction decides disputes between parties where something has gone wrong which the civil law recognizes. The aim is generally to restore the parties to the position they would otherwise have been in by means of damages (money compensation) or injunction (forbidding something), or other order of the court. This jurisdiction is far ranging including breaches of contract, civil wrongs independent of contract or torts such as negligence claims, disputes between landlord and tenant, disputes over liability to pay tax, and divorce and family law.

Enforcement
Awards of damages and court orders can be enforced by the victor by various means including using bailiffs who can seize property, or by ordering registered property such as shares or land to be transferred on the register. Civil courts can ultimately but rarely punish parties for contempt of court where they fail to hand over the subject of a judgement or disobey an injunction.

Which court?
Most civil disputes are heard in the County Court; disputes involving larger sums are heard in the High Court. Almost all civil claims are decided by a judge sitting alone; a notable exception is in defamation cases (libel or slander) where a jury decides whether a person was defamed and also the amount of damages. Huge figures emanate from these cases. In the United States many other civil claims are decided by juries and awards may be large.

Standard of proof
In civil cases the standard of proof is the 'balance of probabilities', in other words: the case is proved if it is more likely than not. This is a different standard to that supposed to be observed in criminal courts. Both civil and criminal cases are conducted under an adversarial system. This means that one of the parties to a dispute must initiate the trial and prove his case. The other must defend it. The system is confrontational, a case may be won by discrediting the opponent's evidence. The court ensures fair play and makes a decision but does not take over the running of any party's case.

Coroner's jurisdiction

Coroners' jurisdiction is different. The Coroner is a judge who inquires into incidents, most often deaths, and pronounces a verdict such as 'Accidental death' or 'Death by misadventure'. He may at his discretion hear evidence of people who wish to be heard but in general he calls his own witnesses who he interrogates, generally in a most gentlemanly manner. Doctors, except those who are already Coroners, are frightened of Coroners. This is on account of critical comments sometimes passed in the course of an inquest in the presence of the press; which can be more important than the verdict itself.

The Coroner's Officer is a policeman who conducts the day to day business of the Coroner and most communication with the Coroner is through him.

Issues of law and issues of fact

The most important part of a trial is usually a dispute over the facts alleged and this is decided by what is called 'the tribunal of fact'. A jury is always this. A judge is often this. Magistrates are supposed to be this. In any trial two principal issues are considered: first, whether the facts alleged are proved and second, whether in law those facts satisfy the requirements to obtain the judgement sought. Matters of procedure and the admissibility of evidence are also questions of law. The law is always a matter for the judge and never for the tribunal of fact. When a judge sits alone he is both tribunal of fact and of law and must keep the two functions separate and distinct. The law is a complex system of principles, only part of which is known to any individual lawyer or judge. Nevertheless everyone is presumed to know the law and his actions are judged accordingly. 'Ignorance of the law is no excuse.'

Proof

In order to win a case before a criminal or civil court almost all facts which make up a party's case have to be proved by evidence. The exception is facts already well known to all judges of which 'judicial notice' is taken. An important example is the ordinary meaning of English words. Judges are also presumed to know the law upon which their decision is founded. Evidence mostly takes the form of oral testimony by a witness under oath. It can also be a document or something real such as a pistol or a bag of 'substances'. As stated above, a higher standard of proof is required of the prosecution in a criminal case. Much of the argument in court is about evidence. Items of evidence have strength or persuasive power which are properly to be weighed in deciding the facts. However in order for the tribunal of fact to hear them they must be admissible, that is they must be lawful evidence. Inadmissible evidence, such as improperly obtained confessions, is not evidence and cannot be heard. In jury trials the judge decides this in the absence of the jury. Hearsay is generally not evidence but there are many exceptions to this rule; furthermore in civil cases the judge hears it at his discretion. Hearsay is something the witness has learnt from another. The rule against hearsay means that a witness may not say what another person has told him as proof of facts even though that other person may be a direct observer of those facts.

Control of the medical profession

The General Medical Council

Under the Medical Act (currently of 1983) the GMC is required to keep the Medical Register. Its professional conduct committee may direct removal of a doctor's registration or suspension or impose a lesser penalty.

After a complaint against a doctor has passed a screening procedure it may come before the professional conduct committee. Its members hear evidence and generally follow the rules of evidence, guided by a legal assessor. Both the prosecution and defence may be represented by lawyers. The committee decides whether the allegations are proved and, if so, whether they amount to serious professional misconduct. Appeals against its decisions are to the Judicial Committee of the Privy Council, which consists of Law Lords.

The 'laws' the professional conduct committee enforces are contained in the four part guide 'Duties of a doctor' and are of fundamental importance to the casualty officer in deciding how to handle difficult situations at work, particularly with respect to his duty of secrecy or confidentiality.

The doctor's employer

Matters of professional conduct or competence may become the concern of a hospital's management who may wish to be released from their contractual obligations to a doctor (sack him). Therefore conduct not serious enough to take a doctor before the GMC may nevertheless place his career in jeopardy. Enquiries by the employing authority must follow procedures communicated in a government circular HC(90)9.

The police

The police forces are bodies of people employed to act as members of a disciplined team. However the legal power of the police over us arises only from the powers of each individual policeman as a citizen, like the rest of us, and from his special powers as a constable. His powers stemmed in the past from the Common Law but now almost entirely from Acts of Parliament. The powers and rights special to a constable, of most significance to the casualty officer, are explained in Chapter 13 and include:

- power of entry into premises
- power of arrest
- power to search people and premises
- power to seize goods including documents
- the right not to be obstructed in the execution of his duty.

Consent

In law the very basis of all we are allowed to do to a patient stems from their agreement that we shall do it. 'The fundamental principle, plain and incontestable, is that every person's body is inviolate'.[1] The law sees consent as a part of everyday affairs and not confined to medical contexts. Note that consent obtained by fraud or deceit is no consent[2] and that no one can consent to an illegal act.[3] Therefore deliberately harming someone including a patient always amounts to the civil wrong of trespass to the person by assault and battery as well as a criminal offence.

Consent requires three elements; the patient must:

(1) have capacity to consent (competence);

(2) understand what he or she is consenting to;

(3) give voluntary consent

It does not have to be signed or in writing and can be implied from actions, such as holding out a limb for an injection.

In some circumstances it is permitted to treat patients without any consent (see below).

Capacity

Adults of sound mind

Adults of sound mind can consent to or refuse treatment, even if the refusal is (objectively) irrational.

> For example Lord Justice Butler-Sloss has said: 'A man or woman of full age and sound understanding may choose to reject medical advice and medical or surgical treatment either partially or in its entirety. A decision to refuse medical treatment by a patient capable of making the decision does not have to be sensible, rational or well-considered'.
>
> (*Re T (adult: refusal of treatment)* [1992] 4 All ER 649 (CA))

Adults of unsound mind

Mentally disordered adults cannot give a valid consent; a person cannot consent to treatment if he is unable to understand its broad nature, purpose, and effects. But if he does understand he can give or refuse consent even though suffering a degree of mental disorder and even if he is a psychiatric in-patient. Lack of understanding may be permanent or temporary, in which case the patient can later recover his capacity to consent.

> A chronic paranoid schizophrenic confined to Broadmoor was able to understand the nature, purpose, and effects of an amputation for ischaemic gangrene and the court found he was therefore competent to refuse the operation he undoubtedly needed.
>
> (*Re C (adult: refusal of treatment)* [1994] 1 WLR 290)

Minors (under 18)

There is no fixed age at which a child becomes able to consent to treatment. By the Family Law Reform Act 1969 any 16 year old of sound mind can consent to treatment (but not to be the subject of research or organ donation). The House of Lords, in the important '*Gillick*' case, made new law and laid down that below sixteen a child can consent to or refuse treatment once mature enough fully to understand the treatment proposed.

In the *Gillick* case Lord Scarman actually said: 'I would hold that as a matter of law, the parental right to determine whether or not their minor child below the age of 16 will have medical treatment terminates if and when the child achieves a sufficient understanding and intelligence to enable him or her to understand fully what is proposed. It will be a question of fact whether a child seeking advice has sufficient understanding of what is involved to give a consent valid in law. Until the child achieves the capacity to consent, the parental right to make the decision continues save only in exceptional circumstances. Emergency, parental neglect, abandonment of the child or inability to find the parent are examples of exceptional situations justifying the doctor proceeding to treat the child without parental knowledge and consent.'

(*Gillick* v. *West Norfolk and Wisbech AHA* [1986] AC 112, [1985] 3 All ER 402)

If a minor refuses treatment the High Court can nevertheless order it.

A 15 year old anorexic was made the subject of an order enabling her to be treated in a specialist unit without her consent. Lord Donaldson, the Master of the Rolls said: 'There can therefore be no doubt that (the court) has power to override the refusal of a minor, whether over the age of 16, or under that age but '*Gillick* competent.'

(*Re W (a minor) (medical treatment)* [1991] 4 All ER 627 (CA))

Lord Donaldson has suggested in the Court of Appeal that even parents can override a '*Gillick* competent' child's refusal.[4] This cannot be right but it may have caused a degree of uncertainty among some lawyers. He is obliged to follow decisions of the House of Lords whose words on the subject (in *Gillick*) are clear.

Understanding

What is needed for consent

Deliberately or recklessly touching a person without their consent can amount to assault and battery which is both a crime and the civil wrong of trespass. Consent allows something to be done which would otherwise be assault and battery. In order to give valid consent to a medical examination or procedure or anything else it is necessary that a person understands only in broad terms the nature of what is going to be done.[6] Consent is about permission. It is not concerned with the quality or suitability of the treatment.

Information, advice, and the duty of care

Over and above simple consent in the above sense, and quite distinct from it, lies the doctor's duty of care to advise a patient properly before obtaining consent to a medical or surgical procedure. If he fails in that duty and the procedure causes harm, the patient may sue in negligence, on the basis he would not have run the risk had he been warned of it. This means that before a procedure a doctor must exercise proper professional skill in advising a patient of its benefits and inherent risks, giving information appropriate to the patient and to the procedure.[7] If he fails in this he is negligent but that does not make the procedure assault and battery (provided he managed to explain in broad terms the nature of the procedure and thus obtained valid consent).

What is 'informed consent'

Indifferent thinking has caused confusion over what a patient needs to know and understand in order to consent. The hybrid doctrine of 'Informed consent' exists in some states of America where a doctor must inform his patient of every single material risk or he commits assault and battery.[5] It ignores the important distinction between consent and the doctor's duty of care. There is no such thing as 'informed consent' in this country although the term has been misunderstood and widely propagated by the medical and nursing press.

Voluntary consent

Consent to or refusal of treatment requires complete freedom of choice. Patients may be under the influence of others; perhaps family members with particular religious beliefs, and the consent or refusal offered may not truly reflect their own wishes.

Guidance was given by the Court of Appeal in *Re T* where an adult, not herself a Jehovah's Witness though brought up in that faith, refused consent to a blood-transfusion in life-threatening circumstances after private conversations with her mother, a member of that sect. The court held that the doctors were right to conclude that T had not been fit to make a valid decision because of her medical condition together with the undue influence of her mother. The court added that in such life-threatening or other serious circumstances where real doubts existed as to the validity of a refusal of consent, doctors and hospital authorities should at once seek the court's assistance and not leave it to other members of the family to make application to the court, as happened in this case.

(*Re T (adult: refusal of medical treatment)* [1992] 4 All ER 649)

The fact that a patient is a prisoner or is institutionalized should make the doctor especially careful to ensure that consent is given freely.[8]

Consent given by others

On behalf of children

The right of parents to decide the fate of their minor children, including medical treatment, has long been recognized. Reflecting modern thinking Parliament renamed that right 'Parental responsibility' in the Children Act 1989.

Parental responsibility

The Children Act 1989 gives 'Parental responsibility' to the following:

(1) Both parents if they have been married at any time since the child's conception.[9]

(2) If the child is illegitimate:
  (a) the mother alone;[10]
  (b) the father also but only if he obtains an order of the court or has the agreement of the mother in prescribed form.[11]

(3) A local authority if the child is in care under a care order.[12]

(4) Others
  (a) if appointed guardian (to care for the child after his parents' death);[13]
  (b) who obtain a residence order (that the child will live with them);[14]
  (c) who adopt a child (thus extinguishing the rights of the natural parents);
  (d) who obtain an emergency protection order (usually the local authority).

More than one person, including the local authority, can have parental responsibility at the same time. Any person with parental responsibility can alone give consent without consulting the others provided this is not in contravention of any court order.[15]

The Children Act of 1989 also provides that persons who 'have care of the child' may 'do what is reasonable' to safeguard or promote the child's welfare.[16] This awaits interpretation but may mean schoolmasters, childminders, and the like are able to consent to treatment.

On behalf of adults

Nobody else can give consent on behalf of an adult under any circumstances whatever his mental state. Getting relatives to sign a consent form has no effect and serves no purpose.

For example Lord Goff referred to '. . . incompetent adults, on whose behalf nobody has power to give consent to medical treatment'.

(*Airdale NHS Trust* v. *Bland* [1993] 1 All ER 821)

When physical conditions may be treated without consent

Application of the doctrine of necessity

This important question was settled by the House of Lords in 1989 in *Re F*. Where an adult lacks the capacity to consent, whether temporarily or permanently, he may lawfully be given treatment 'in his best interests'. Relatives and other carers should be consulted if possible. The treatment must be in accordance with a responsible and competent body of medical opinion. If the incapacity is temporary then after necessary emergency treatment the patient should be allowed to recover and decide long-term measures.

When psychiatric conditions may be treated without consent

The Mental Health Act 1983 sections 2 and 3 allows patients to be detained and treated for mental illness against their will. This treatment can include necessary ancillary physical treatment such as treating the physical consequences of a suicide attempt or force-feeding an anorexic patient.[17] The Mental Health Act does not otherwise permit physical treatment against a person's will.

In *Re F*, a 36 year old woman with the mental age of a
small child had formed a sexual relationship with a male
patient. The staff considered it undesirable to restrict her
movements and that she would not be able to cope with
pregnancy or childbirth. No form of contraception was
suitable and the hospital and her mother wished her steril-
ized.

They sought a court declaration that the proposed operation would be lawful without the patient's consent, which
she could not give. The House of Lords agreed she could
have the operation and explained the common law principle at length including the following words:

'The operation or other treatment will be in their best
interests if, but only if, it is carried out in order either to
save their lives, or to ensure improvement or prevent
deterioration in their physical or mental health.' (Lord
Brandon)

'In making decisions about treatment the doctor must
act in accordance with a responsible and competent body
of relevant professional opinion on the principles set out
in *Bolam* v. *Friern Hospital Management Committee* . . . It
must surely be good practice to consult relatives and
others who are concerned with the care of the patient.'
(Lord Goff)

'Where, for example, a surgeon performs an operation
without his consent on a patient temporarily rendered
unconscious in an accident, he should do no more than is
reasonably required, in the best interests of the patient,
before he recovers consciousness . . . the patient is
expected before long to regain consciousness and can
then be consulted about longer term measures.' . . .
'But where the state of affairs is permanent or semi-
permanent, as may be so in the case of a mentally disordered person, there is no point in waiting to obtain the
patient's consent.' (Lord Goff)

(*Re F. (mental patient: sterilization)* [1989] 2 WLR 1025
(CA,HL))

End notes

1. Words of Lord Justice Robert Goff in *Collins* v. *Wilcock* [1984] 1 WLR 1172

2. The famous case of *R* v. *Williams* [1923] 1 KB 340 (CCA) in which a singing teacher had sexual intercourse with a 16 year old girl under the pretence that it was an operation to improve her voice. Held: it was no consent and the act was rape.
   See also *R* v. *Case* (1850) 1 Den 580 where a quack doctor obtained consent by fraud for the same purpose.

3. 'Consent is no defence where severe blows are given for the purpose of gratifying perverted sexual passion', *R* v. *Donovan* [1934] 2 KB 498.
   This principle was again applied in *R* v. *Brown* [1993] 2 WLR 556 where the victims 'consented' to (illegal) acts of homosexual sadism.

4. *Re R* (a minor)(wardship: medical treatment) [1991] 4 All ER 177. [1992] Fam 11 (CA)

5. e.g. *Canterbury* v. *Spence* 464 F 2d 772 (1972).

6. *Chatterton* v. *Gerson* [1981] QB 432, [1981] 1 All ER 257 [QBD)

7. *Sidaway* v. *Governors of the Bethlem Royal Hospital and the Maudsley Hospital* [1985] AC 871, [1985] 1 All ER 643 (HL)

8. *Freeman* v. *Home Office* (No 2) [1984] QB 542, [1984] 1 All ER 1036 (CA)

9. Children Act 1989 S.29(1); Family Law Reform Act 1987 s.1(2)

10. Children Act 1989 s.2(2)

11. Children Act 1989 s.4(1) or s.12(1)

12. Children Act 1989 s.33(3)(a)

13. Children Act 1989 s.5(6)

14. Children Act 1989 s.12(2)

15. Children Act 1989 s.2(7,8)

16. Children Act 1989 s.3(5)

17. Mental Health Act 1983 s.63; *B* v. *Croydon Health Authority* [1995] 2 WLR 294.

CHAPTER 11

Medical negligence and vicarious liability

• **Medical negligence 118** • **Vicarious liability 122**

The civil law exists to redress wrongs, not to punish wrong-doers. It is principally concerned with parties who fall out over business agreements, children and property of families who fall apart, and with those who commit and those who suffer civil wrongs (or torts). In National Health Service work there are no contracts between doctors and patients and so the bulk of medical litigation is in the realm of tort. In the past it was commonly in the form of an action for trespass to the person where it was not necessary to prove that damage was caused to the victim.[1] This method is still available in cases where treatment has been given without consent,[2] for example, mistakenly circumcising a patient who had consented to tonsillectomy. Nowadays however medical litigation is based on the tort of negligence.[3]

Medical negligence

The elements of negligence

For a plaintiff to obtain damages in negligence from a defendant he must prove:

(1) that the defendant owed him a duty of care;[4]

(2) that he failed in that duty;

(3) that damage was suffered, caused by that failure.

The term 'negligence' has no absolute connection with the tort and does not even properly describe it. Unfortunately the word makes defendants take litigation personally rather than seeing it through lawyers' eyes, as a means of compensation for loss.[5] It has been suggested we adopt a no-fault system of compensation for certain forms of loss. If this came about it would mean that victims of accidents would be compensated without having to prove want of care by the defendant.

Lord Wright said: '. . . Negligence means more than heedless or careless conduct . . .; it properly connotes the complex concept of duty, breach and damage thereby suffered by the person to whom the duty was owing.'

(*Lochgelly Iron Co* v. *M'Mullan* [1934] AC1)

An example of an action in negligence is the consequence of a motor accident where a driver runs into another's car. A driver owes a legal duty to take reasonable care of other road users. If he fails to take such care (or is 'negligent') the second element is satisfied. If that want of care results in damage to another vehicle then he is liable to put its owner in the same position as if the accident had not occurred. The situation may be complicated by the victim being partly to blame. That is recognized as contributory negligence and the award of damages reduced in proportion to the victim's share of the fault. An example is the injured passenger who failed to wear his seat belt.

It goes without saying that a doctor owes a duty of care to someone he accepts as a patient. Much expensive legal intellect has considered the scope of that duty. It may be easily definable in a case where a doctor has been blatantly indifferent to the care of his patient. It is more difficult when what is alleged is a wrong decision or wrong action due to lack of professional skill. The duty was lucidly set out in 1957 in the *Bolam* case.

A patient was given electro-convulsive therapy without relaxant drugs and suffered bilateral stove-in acetabular fractures. The plaintiff claimed that the doctor was negligent in failing (*inter alia*) to administer relaxant drugs. The court heard evidence from several distinguished experts whose opinions differed. At the date of the treatment some would relax their patient, others would not.

The case was before a jury and in his address to the jury Mr Justice McNair said:

'I must tell you what in law we mean by "negligence" . . . where you get a situation which involves the use of some special skill or competence . . . The test is the standard of the ordinary skilled man exercising and professing to have that special skill. A man need not possess the highest expert skill; it is well established law that it is sufficient if he exercises the ordinary skill of an ordinary competent man exercising that particular art'.

He went on to say '. . . He is not guilty of negligence if he has acted in accordance with a practice accepted as proper by a responsible body of medical men skilled in that particular art.'

The jury found the doctor was not negligent.

(*Bolam v. Friern Hospital Management Committee* [1957] 1 WLR 582)

These words remain pure and unsullied and authoritative despite attempts to alter them. They have been repeatedly applied by the House of Lords and the Court of Appeal.

Inexperience

It is essential that beginners in medicine realize they are responsible for all that they do and appreciate their own limitations.

What is the standard of care expected of a junior or inexperienced doctor? It is not absolutely settled but is probably the same as that of a trained doctor in that specialty. However the duty may be discharged by referring to a senior.

A learner driver struck a lamp post, damaging it and the instructor's patella. The instructor sued and lost but successfully appealed to the Court of Appeal where Lord Justice Denning said: 'It requires of him the same standard or care as any other driver . . . the learner driver may be doing his best but his incompetent best is not good enough'.

(*Nettleship* v. *Weston* [1971] 2 QB 691 (CA))

This question was considered in *Wilsher* v. *Essex AHA* but the law on this issue was unfortunately left uncertain. A premature baby in a special care baby unit was given high doses of oxygen due to a junior doctor inadvertently placing the monitoring catheter via the umbilical vein instead of an artery. The plaintiff sued for his damaged eyesight and was awarded £116 199. The authority appealed to the Court of Appeal where the judges made relevant but conflicting remarks in their judgements.

Lord Justice Mustill said: 'To my mind, this notion of a duty tailored to the actor rather than to the act, has no place in the law of tort'.

Lord Justice Glidewell said: 'In my view the law requires the trainee or learner to be judged by the same standard as his more experienced colleagues. If this test appears unduly harsh in relation to the inexperienced doctor, called on to exercise a specialist skill will, as part of that skill, seek the advice and help of his superiors when he does or may need it. If he does seek such help, he will often have satisfied the test, even though he may himself have made a mistake'.

Sir Nicholas Browne-Wilkinson, Vice-Chancellor (dissenting) said: 'A doctor . . . should only be held liable for acts or omissions which a careful doctor with his qualifications and experience would not have done or omitted'.

(*Wilsher* v. *Essex AHA* [1987] QB 730, [1986] 3 All ER 801 (CA))

> The standard expected of a casualty officer was recently considered in the High Court. The majority view of Lords Justice Glidewell and Mustill in Wilsher (above) was followed, more or less.
>
> A casualty officer of four months' experience was found to have taken an inadequate history and made an inadequate examination of an adult with spitting and pooling of saliva who turned out to have epiglottitis and later developed airway obstruction causing severe brain damage.
>
> It was said that the standard was 'that of a reasonably competent senior houseman acting as a casualty officer without any reference to the length of experience.'
>
> (*Djemal* v. *Bexley Health Authority* [1995] 6 Med LR 269)

Vicarious liability

This word means literally 'substituted' liability whereby a master is liable for the torts of his servants in the course of their employment. (In ecclesiastical language a vicar is a substitute for another). In law the master (the employing authority) and his servant (the doctor) are both liable in full for the whole amount of damage caused by the servant's want of care. The fact that a doctor is an independent professional, whose employer can tell him what to do but not how to do it, does not absolve the employer from its own duty of care.

> A labourer went into hospital for the treatment of Dupuytren's contracture of two fingers. He was operated on and splinted for 14 days. On removal of the splint, the operated fingers were bent and stiff and the other two fingers on the hand were affected.
>
> He sued and lost on the ground that he had failed to prove negligence in any member of the hospital's staff. His appeal to the Court of Appeal was successful on the basis that the hospital itself owed its patients a duty of care.
>
> Lord Justice Denning said 'In my opinion, authorities who run a hospital, be they local authorities, government

boards, or any other corporation, are in law under the self same duty as the humblest doctor. Whenever they accept a patient for treatment, they must use reasonable care and skill to cure him of his ailment. The hospital authorities cannot of course do it by themselves. They have no ears to listen through the stethoscope, and no hands to hold the knife. They must do it by the staff which they employ, and, if their staff are negligent in giving the treatment, they are just as liable for that negligence as is anyone else who employs others to do his duties for him'.

(*Cassidy* v. *Ministry of Health* [1951] 2 KB 343)

Both a doctor and his employing authority are liable in full for the doctor's failure to take proper care of his patients. This only applies to actions in the course of his employment and so would not include negligence in treating, for example, a roadside case. The same applies to nurses and their employers.

On 1st January 1990 the NHS Indemnity Scheme came into existence. A government circular[5] instructed health authorities that they were also responsible for the handling and financing of claims of negligence against their medical and dental staff in the course of their NHS employment. Previously an agreement had existed between the Department of Health and the defence societies whereby employers paid half the damages and the doctors paid the other half, through their defence societies.

End notes

1. e.g. *Cull* v. *Royal Surrey County Hospital* [1932] 1 BMJ 1195
2. *Hills* v. *Potter* [1983] 3 All ER 716
3. *Chatterton* v. *Gerson* [1981] QB 432
4. *Donoghue* v. *Stephenson* [1932] AC 562
5. Claims of Medical Negligence Against Hospitals and Community Doctors and Dentists (HC(89)34)

Further reading:

Lewis, C. J. (1992) *Medical negligence* (2nd ed). Tolley Publishing Co.

CHAPTER 12

Confidentiality

- The ethical obligation 124 • The legal obligation 130

The doctor's obligation of secrecy is ancient, and embedded in the Hippocratic Oath: 'I will keep silence thereon, counting such things to be as sacred secrets'. It is essential to the trust between doctors and patients. It is a legal as well as an ethical obligation and can be enforced by the courts. The principal means of enforcement is by complaint to the General Medical Council which has draconian powers including erasure from the Medical Register. Nurses are subject to similar discipline by their professional body.

As this is a book of law and not ethics, the GMCs guidance is here quoted incompletely. The original should be consulted on questions of medical ethics.

The ethical obligation

This is set out in *Duties of a Doctor: Confidentiality* (hereafter called the yellow book) published by the GMC in October 1995.

Effect of death
A patient's death does not release a doctor from the obligation to maintain confidentiality. (yellow book para 13)

Exceptions to the ethical obligation

The GMC's guidance lists circumstances:
(1) where a doctor **may** properly disclose information and

> 'Patients have a right to expect that you will not disclose any personal information which you learn during the course of your professional duties, unless they give permission'
>
> and
>
> 'When you are responsible for confidential information you must make sure that the information is effectively protected against improper disclosure when it is disposed of, stored, transmitted or received.
>
> (yellow book para 1)

(2) when the law requires a doctor **must** disclose information, to which the GMC gives 'ethical blessing'.

When the doctor may disclose information

Doctors are permitted to disclose information in the following circumstances:

Consent

Consent by the patient or 'a person properly authorized to act on the patient's behalf'

(See yellow book para 2 which unfortunately does not explain 'properly authorized' nor who can do the proper authorizing.)

To members of a health care team

> 'Modern medical practice usually involves teams of doctors, other health care workers, and sometimes people from outside the health care professions . . . it is often essential to pass confidential information between members of the team'.
>
> (yellow book para 3)
>
> 'All medical members of a team have a duty to make sure that other team members understand and observe confidentiality'.
>
> (yellow book para 8)

In the patient's medical interests

> '. . . if you consider that a patient is incapable of giving consent to treatment because of immaturity, illness, or mental incapacity, and you have tried unsuccessfully to persuade the patient to allow an appropriate person to be involved in the consultation . . . You must tell the patient before disclosing any information'.
>
> (yellow book para 10)
>
> '. . . you may judge that seeking consent to disclosure of confidential information would be damaging to the patient . . . For example . . . that a close relative should know about the patient's terminal condition. . .'
>
> (yellow book para 12)
>
> 'If you believe a patient to be a victim of neglect or physical or sexual abuse, and unable to give or withhold consent to disclosure, you should usually give information to an appropriate responsible person or statutory agency, in order to prevent further harm to the patient'.
>
> (yellow book para 11)

It is seldom that such difficult situations arise exclusively within an emergency department and referral of the patient to a specialist within the hospital is suggested. When this is not possible such decisions must be taken by a senior and experienced doctor. They are likely to be criticized.

In teaching, research, and audit
The disclosure of information is subject to the permission of any patient who can be identified (yellow book paras 15 and 17). Disclosure is also now permitted if a research ethics committee decides public interest in the research outweighs patients' right to confidentiality. (yellow book para 16)

In the interests of others

> 'Disclosures may be necessary in the public interest where a failure to disclose information may expose the patient, or others, to risk of death or serious harm. In such circum-

stances you should disclose information promptly to an appropriate person or authority . . . for example, where: 'a patient continues to drive against medical advice. . .' 'A colleague, who is also a patient, is placing patients at risk as a result of illness. . .
'Disclosure is necessary for the prevention or detection of a serious crime'.

(yellow book paras 18 and 19)

As a matter of law as well as ethics a doctor's duty of confidentiality is not absolute.

Lord Justice Bingham said in *W* v. *Edgell* [1990] (see also below) 'The law recognises an important public interest in maintaining professional duties of confidence; but . . . the law treats such duties not as absolute but as liable to be overridden where there is held to be a stronger public interest in disclosure'.

Notice the narrow circumstances referred to in the GMCs advice as well as in the cases referred to at the end. Pressure may be exerted on accident and emergency staff to disclose information on patients suspected of serious offences such as robbery, burglary, or dealing in drugs. There is now no legal obligation to do so. (Failing to report a felony constituted the offence of Misprision of Felony until it was abolished in 1967.) There may nevertheless be a moral obligation to do so and it may be the correct course of action in extreme circumstances.

Never give misleading information to the Police (as opposed to declining to give information). This would amount to the criminal offence of obstructing a police officer in the execution of his duty (Police Act 1964 section 51 (3)).

In proceedings before a committee of the GMC
The patient's consent is still required in this situation. (yellow book para 22)

A patient instructed a consultant psychiatrist to prepare an independent report for use at a Mental Health Review Tribunal. The report was unfavourable to the patient who withdrew his application to the tribunal and refused to consent to the doctor disclosing the report. The consultant nevertheless disclosed the report and was sued for breach of confidence. The circumstances were extreme as the patient had shot dead five people under the disability of a serious mental illness and the consultant considered there was a real risk of consequent danger to the public if a decision in relation to the patient came to be made on the basis of inadequate information. The patient's claim was unsuccessful, 'Dr Edgell was clearly justified in taking the course that he did.'

(*W* v. *Edgell* [1990] 1 Ch 359)

A patient, who was a defendant in criminal proceedings for attempted murder, instructed a consultant psychiatrist to prepare a report. That psychiatrist discovered the defence lawyers were not going to show his report to the court. He decided to draw it to the attention of the prosecution who informed the judge. It was held that the strong public interest in the disclosure of the doctor's view that the patient would continue to be a danger to the public overrode his duty of confidence and that he had acted reasonably and responsibly.

(*R* v. *Crozier* [1990] 12 Cr App Rep)

When the doctor must disclose information

These are the **only** circumstances in which the law requires disclosure.

Order of a court
It is contempt of court for a witness in open court to refuse to answer a question put to him by the judge. A doctor is in the

same position as any other witness. The yellow book permits a doctor to disclose information after establishing the extent of what is needed and after making known any objections to the proposed disclosure. (yellow book para 20)

Requirements imposed by statute
Certain Acts of Parliament require a doctor to disclose information about a patient. The GMC gives its permission to do this. (yellow book para 20)

A. Statute requiring disclosure when demanded

Drivers
The Road Traffic Act 1988 s.172 (2) to (4) requires disclosure to the police of information leading to the identification of a driver involved in a traffic offence. Failure to do so is itself a criminal offence.[1]

B. Statutes imposing a positive duty to report

Terrorism
By the Prevention of Terrorism (Temporary Provisions) Act 1989 s.18 it is an offence to fail to report to the Police information which might assist in preventing an act of terrorism or apprehending a terrorist connected with Northern Ireland.

Drug addicts
The Misuse of Drugs (Notification and supply to Addicts) Regulations 1973 made under the Misuse of Drugs Act 1971 require a doctor attending a person he suspects is addicted to:

Cocaine	Methadone
Dextromoramide	Morphine
Diamorphine	Opium
Dipipanone	Oxycodone
Hydrocodone	Pethidine
Hydromorphone	Phenazocine
Levorphanol	Piritramide

to give written particulars of that person to the Home Office.[2]

Some infectious diseases
The Public Health (Infectious Diseases) Act 1984 sections 10 and 11 impose an obligation on any doctor to report a patient to the proper officer of the local authority if he suspects they have:

cholera	smallpox
plague	typhus
relapsing fever	food poisoning

It is an offence to fail to do this.

The legal obligation

Legal remedies for improper disclosure

Breach of duty

If a doctor threatens improperly to reveal confidences there is no doubt that an injunction would be granted preventing disclosure. Although there is no English legal decision directly on the point there is no shortage of authority on the protection of confidences generally and there is no doubt that a doctor owes a legal duty of confidence.[3,4] If he did improperly reveal confidences and the patient suffered damage as a result it is probable the patient could not only invoke the disciplinary powers of the GMC but also sue the doctor for damages in an action for breach of the duty of confidence.[5]

Under the contract of employment

When a hospital authority takes on an employee it is often made a term of the contract of employment that he shall keep secret anything learnt about a patient in the course of that employment. Such a contractual duty is undoubtedly enforceable and provides the employer with firm grounds for dismissal of a leaker. However a term of a contract cannot be enforced if contrary to the public interest. It seems unlikely that the courts would prevent doctors disclosing confidences when it was ethically proper to do so.

End notes

1. *Hunter* v. *Mann* [1974] QB 767, [1974] 2 All ER 414 (DC) see Chapter 4 (p. 66)
2. Chief Medical Officer, Home Office, Drugs Branch, Queen Anne's Gate, London SW1H 9AT, within 7 days to include name and address, sex, date of birth, NHS number if known, date of attendance, whether the person injects any drug

3. For example *Attorney General* v. *Guardian Newspapers Limited* (No 2) [1990] 1 AC 109 (The Spycatcher case)
4. and see *Goddard* v. *Nationwide Building Society* [1986] 3 All ER 264 and *W* v. *Edgell* at 389 and 419
5. *Furniss* v. *Fitchett* [1958] NZLR 396, a case directly on this point but being a New Zealand case of only persuasive authority in England

Further reading

General Medical Council, October 1995. *Duties of a Doctor.*

Police powers

The law of England and the British Constitution developed with traditions of the rights of man and the liberty of the subject. These have been eroded as governments have sought to protect us from antisocial and lawless elements, in part by conferring special powers on police constables. It is fundamental that a constable has no general or inherent power to enter premises, detain people, seize things, or obtain answers to his questions. He can only do any of these by exercising a specific power given him by statute or developed in the common law. Most of these powers were abolished by the Police and Criminal Evidence Act 1984 (PACE) and new ones created in their place. They include powers of: stop and search, entry, and arrest. Those most relevant to emergency department practice are summarized below.

PACE codes of practice

The Home Secretary is required by the act to issue codes of practice for constables exercising their powers. They are approved by Parliament. Breach of the codes may result in a judge excluding evidence and in disciplinary proceedings against the police officer. One part relevant to emergency departments is code C 14.2: 'If a person is in police detention at a hospital he may not be questioned without the agreement of a responsible doctor'.

No legal requirement to give any information to the police

This has been mentioned in Chapter 12 (confidentiality p. 127). In *Rice* v. *Connelly* (below) this important principle was affirmed. The PACE code of practice refers to this: 'This code does not affect the principle that all citizens have a duty to help police officers to prevent crime and to discover offenders. This is a civic rather than a legal duty . . .' (Note 1.B, code C).

This principle is subject to two statutory exceptions requiring information leading to (a) the identity of a driver involved in a traffic offence and (b) concerning terrorists connected with Northern Ireland.

A constable thought Mr Rice was acting suspiciously. When asked for his name and address he refused to answer any of the constable's questions. He was charged with obstructing the constable in the execution of his duty. The magistrates court convicted him but on appeal it was held that, while every citizen has a moral or social duty to assist the police, there was no legal duty. In refusing to answer the questions Mr Rice had not obstructed the constable.

The Lord Chief Justice, Lord Parker said: 'In my judgement, there is all the difference in the world between deliberately telling a false story, something which on no view a citizen has a right to do, and preserving silence or refusing to answer, something which he has every right to do.'

(*Rice* v. *Connelly* [1966] 2 QB 414, [1966] 2 All ER 649)

Obstructing a constable in the execution of his duty

Policemen sometimes threaten to charge people with this and its exact scope is relevant. S.51(3) of the Police Act 1964 provides: 'Any person who resists or wilfully obstructs a constable in the execution of his duty shall be guilty of an offence and liable on summary conviction to imprisonment for a term not exceeding one month or to a fine . . .'

'*Wilfully*' means doing it on purpose, not carelessly or by accident'.

'*Obstructs*' has been defined in *Hinchliffe* v. *Sheldon*[1] as 'making it more difficult for the police to carry out their duties'. Examples are: warning offenders so they avoid being caught, preventing a constable exercising his legal power of entry, preventing him performing a duty such as by making a breath test unworkable by further drinking. Telling police a false story is obstruction but refusing to answer questions is certainly not, even though that makes it more difficult for the police to carry out their duties.

'*In the execution of his duty*' means carrying out his lawful functions. This includes the ordinary duties of preventing and detecting crime, arresting offenders, and keeping the peace. A constable is normally entitled to ask questions of anyone. However he is not in the execution of his duty if he is a trespasser; he becomes one on being asked to leave (unless exercising his legal power of entry).

Powers of arrest without warrant

Arrest involves depriving a person of liberty to go where he pleases. It can be by words or by force but must be quite clear and the reason given. The person arrested must be taken to a designated police station as soon as practicable.

Arrestable offence

'Arrestable offence' has a complex definition (PACE s.24) but essentially means any offence for which the penalty is five years imprisonment or more plus certain miscellaneous offences.

Anyone may arrest:

- someone who is committing an arrestable offence or someone he has grounds to suspect is committing an arrestable offence;
- someone guilty of the offence where an arrestable offence has actually been committed, or someone whom he has reasonable grounds to suspect is guilty of it.

Only a constable may arrest:

- someone who is about to commit or whom he suspects is about to commit an arrestable offence;
- someone he suspects to be guilty of an arrestable offence that he suspects has been committed (even though no offence has actually been committed).

Other offences: the general arrest conditions[2]

(These apply to situations where Parliament has deemed a summons unsuitable for getting the offender to court.)

A **constable** who suspects **any** offence has been committed or attempted may arrest any person he suspects if one of the general arrest conditions is fulfilled. These include:

- inability to verify name and address
- avoidance of injury to the person or loss of or damage to property
- protection of a child or other vulnerable person
- some offences against public decency
- obstructing the highway.

Other circumstances

Breach of the peace

A **constable** has power at common law to arrest without warrant any person he sees breaking the peace or behaving so as to cause him to apprehend a breach of the peace. Where a breach occurs a constable may call on anybody for assistance and they must give that assistance. Once the breach has ended the power of arrest ceases.

What is a breach of the peace? There is no authoritative definition.[3] It includes fighting. It must be related to violence.

There is a breach whenever harm is done or likely to be done to a person or his property in his presence. A mere threat of it is not enough.

Public Order Act 1986: offences of disorder
This statute gives a constable powers of arrest without warrant for some offences often committed in emergency departments including, for example:

- affray (using or threatening violence, by more than mere words, in a way that would cause someone of reasonable firmness to fear for his safety); and

- fear and provocation of violence (using threatening abusive or insulting words or behaviour towards someone, intending them to believe violence will immediately be used or else intending to provoke violence by them. A constable may arrest anyone he has reasonable grounds to suspect of having committed these offences in public or private places (including emergency departments).

Powers of entry, search, and seizure

In some circumstances the police have a legal right to enter an emergency department and take things.

Without a search warrant[4]

A constable may enter and search premises:

- to arrest someone for an arrestable offence or for whom there is a warrant for arrest if he has reasonable grounds to believe the person is there;

- to recapture someone who has escaped from the police, court, prison, or compulsory psychiatric admission;

- to save life or limb or prevent serious damage to property;

- to deal with or prevent a breach of the peace.

There are some miscellaneous statutory powers of entry other than to make an arrest; e.g. Misuse of Drugs Act 1971 s.23(1) enables a constable to enter the premises of a producer or supplier of controlled drugs and inspect the relevant books and stock. This would obviously apply to an emergency department.

With a search warrant

A magistrate may issue a warrant to a constable to enter premises and search for evidence and seize it.[5] He must first be satisfied certain conditions are fulfilled including that a 'serious arrestable offence'[6] has been committed and that the material sought is not 'excluded material'. Medical records will fall within the definition of excluded material (see below) so that emergency departments will be unlikely to encounter demands for such material supported by a search warrant.

By order of a circuit judge

As mentioned above a Magistrate may not issue a search warrant in respect of 'excluded material'. Medical records and human tissue and tissue fluid taken for diagnosis or treatment are within the definition of excluded material.[13] Only a Circuit Judge may make an order for the production of such material and the judge may only make such an order in the very limited circumstances in which a search warrant could have been granted to seek such material under old (pre-PACE) statutes, such as a search for stolen goods including stolen medical records (s.26 Theft Act 1968).

Excluded material
This is defined in PACE s.11(1):

(a) personal records which a person has acquired or created in the course of any trade, business, profession or other occupation or for the purposes of any paid or unpaid office and which he holds in confidence.

(b) human tissue or tissue fluid which has been taken for the purposes of diagnosis or medical treatment and which a person holds in confidence. . .

PACE s.12 . . . 'personal records' means documentary and other records concerning an individual (whether living or dead) who can be identified from them, and relating—(a) to his physical or mental health. . .

It is important to understand that an Order made by a Circuit Judge in these circumstances, even in error, is only made after the parties have had the opportunity of being heard, so that the doctor or hospital authority will be given notice of the application by the police and will have an opportunity of being heard by the Circuit Judge. In only one circumstance is an order likely to be made without such notice and this is where an application is made by the police in the course of investigating acts of terrorism.[7]

For all practical purposes therefore the police are effectively excluded from access to medical records except in cases of terrorist investigation or, at least, in circumstances where the hospital will have had notice that an application will be made. Even then an order will only be granted in closely controlled circumstances.

Powers of stop and search

In the emergency department context this means 'detain and search'. A constable can search someone he has reasonable grounds to suspect has prohibited things on him.

For offensive weapons, stolen goods, and items for use in stealing

PACE s.1 enables a constable to stop and search someone on whom he has reasonable grounds to suspect he will find these things if that person is in a place to which a section of the public has access (including an emergency department).

For controlled drugs

The Misuse of Drugs Act 1971 (s.23 (2)) gives a constable power to stop and search any person he reasonably suspects of unlawfully possessing controlled drugs.

For firearms

The Firearms Act 1968 s.47 gives a constable power to enter any place and search a person for a firearm if he suspects him of having it in a public place (including an emergency department).

End notes

1. [1955] 1 WLR 1207. [1955] 3 All ER 406
2. PACE s.25 and Schedule 2
3. *Timothy* v. *Simpson* (1835) 1 Cr M & R 757, 4 LJMC 73
   R v. *Howell* [1982] QB 416 [1981] 3 All ER 383 (CA)
   Ingle v. *Bell* (1836) 1 M & W 516, 5 LJMC 85
4. PACE s.17
5. PACE s.8
6. A 'serious arrestable offence' includes: treason, murder, manslaughter, rape, kidnapping, incest with a girl under 13, buggery with a boy under 16 or a person who has not consented, indecent assaults by men upon men. Also causing explosions likely to endanger life or property, intercourse with a girl under 13, certain criminal uses of firearms, hostage taking, hi-jacking, torture, causing death by dangerous driving or by careless driving under the influence of drink or drugs. Also certain drug trafficking offences, certain terrorist offences and any other arrestable offence leading to serious consequences; serious harm to the security of the state or public order, serious interference with the administration of justice or the investigation of offences, death, serious injury, substantial financial gain or serious financial loss. (PACE s.116)
7. Prevention of Terrorism (Temporary Provisions) Act 1989, Sch7, para 31

Controlled drugs

Emergency department staff handle controlled drugs so often they may give little thought to the risks. The inevitable arrival of addicts at emergency departments and their attendant warring bands of 'unlicensed pharmacists' place staff at risk of exceeding their privileges and having their actions questioned. A police or other investigation into a doctor's or nurse's handling of controlled drugs may result in suspension by an employer, other damage to a career or, at worst, a prison sentence. This section outlines part of the law on misuse of drugs.

The principal crimes

The present statutory basis of drug abuse control is the Misuse of Drugs Act 1971 (MDA) and the Home Secretary's regulations made under s.7 of it. The present regulations are those of 1985. The Act and regulations are confusing to lawyers and incomprehensible to laymen.

The MDA puts a blanket prohibition on possession and supply of controlled substances and then makes various exceptions and defences. The regulations also set out the circumstances under which certain classes of people can lawfully possess or supply them.

The crime of possession

Section 5(2) of the MDA says '. . .it is an offence for a person to have a controlled drug in his possession. . .'
Possession consists of:

(1) having the item in physical custody or control;
and

(2) knowing of the existence of the item (or could reasonably have known of it); and

(3) the item must be a controlled drug.

'*Knowing*' is so interpreted that a mistake as to the 'quality and nature' of the substance, e.g. thinking it was aspirin when it was heroin, does not prevent possession of it being unlawful.

A person who picked up about fifty discarded cigarette ends, without knowing that three of them contained cannabis mixed with the tobacco, was held to be in unlawful possession. His mistake didn't count.

Searle v. *Randolph* [1972] Crim LR 779 (DC)

On the other hand if it were believed to be an item of a 'wholly different nature' such as scent rather than amphetamine this might not amount to unlawful possession.[1]

The crimes of (a) supply and (b) possession with intent to supply

Section 4(3)(a) of the MDA says
'. . .it is an offence for a person to supply or offer to supply a controlled drug to another. . .'
Section 5(3) says
'. . .it is an offence for a person to have a controlled drug in his possession, whether lawfully or not, with intent to supply it to another. . .'
'*Supply*' means the transfer of physical control of a controlled drug to another with the intention of enabling the recipient to use that drug for his own purposes. For example where a person has hold of another's drugs and returns them. Someone

who deposits his drugs for safe keeping does not himself commit the offence of supply.

A registered addict went into a lavatory to inject some of his methadone. He left the rest with his wife to hold. The court found this did not amount to supplying her since only physical control of it was transferred.

(*R* v. *Dempsey* (1986) 82 Cr App R 291)

But a person who keeps the drugs for someone intending to return them does commit the offence of possession with intent to supply.

A package of cannabis resin was found by police in the accused's car. The package had been left there by a friend who was to collect it. The House of Lords held the accused was guilty because he intended to return it for the friend's benefit.

(*R* v. *Maginnis* [1987] AC 303)

If he does in fact return them he is also guilty of unlawfully supplying them to their owner. The illogical situation exists where a mere caretaker is in a worse position than the owner of drugs.

An accused person will be acquitted as usual if the prosecution cannot prove all the necessary elements of the offence, for example, knowledge of the existence of a package.

Special statutory defences to these charges

Lack of knowledge: MDA s.28
Section 28 of the MDA creates additional special defences for persons accused of the above offences. However to use them the accused must prove the facts on which they are based.

(i) Ignorance of facts: MDA s.28(2)
'Subject to subsection 3 below . . . it shall be a defence for the accused to prove that he neither knew of nor suspected nor

had reason to suspect the existence of some fact alleged by the prosecution. . .'

To be acquitted the accused must prove not only that he didn't know or suspect but also that he had no reason to suspect. This is an objective test and so he is judged on what he ought to have believed.

(ii) Ignorance of the nature of the drug MDA s.28(3)

'. . .the accused

(a) **shall not be acquitted** . . . by reason only of proving that he neither knew of nor suspected nor had reason to suspect that the substance or product in question was the **particular controlled drug** alleged, but

(b) **shall be acquitted**

- if he proves that he neither knew of nor suspected nor had reason to suspect that the substance or product in question was a controlled drug, or

- if he proves that he believed the substance or product in question to be a controlled drug . . . such that, if it had in fact been that controlled drug . . . he would not . . . have been committing any offence.'

This means that a person cannot say in his defence that he knew he had a controlled drug but thought it was a different one to that found on him, unless it would have been no offence to have that different one. In other words he believed he was carrying a controlled drug from a different schedule.

For example where the controlled drug found on him is prohibited, like heroin, but he believed it was a permitted controlled drug, such as valium, he has the defence and will be acquitted. The same applies to a doctor who, in the course of his duty, comes into possession of what he believes is heroin (which he may possess) but which turns out to be cannabis (which he may not).

Destruction or surrender of drugs: MDA s.5(4)
Section 5(4) says:
'. . .it shall be a defence for him to prove:

(a) . . .he took possession of it for the purpose of preventing another from committing or continuing to commit an offence in connection with that drug, and

as soon as possible . . . he took all such steps as were reasonably open to him to destroy the drug or to deliver it into the custody of a person lawfully entitled to take custody of it; or

(b) . . .he took possession of it for the purpose of delivering it into the custody of a person lawfully entitled to take custody of it, and

as soon as possible . . . he took all such steps as were reasonably open to him to deliver it into the custody of such a person'

This section enables someone to confiscate a controlled drug and either destroy it or give it to the police. Destruction of the drug is only permitted when an offence is actually being committed, not when merely suspected, so the lawful drugs of a registered addict may not be destroyed.

'Lawfully entitled to take custody'
It has not been decided who exactly is 'lawfully entitled to take custody' but it probably means a constable or customs officer rather than one of those 'who may lawfully have that drug in their possession' such as doctors or pharmacists. In any case a schedule 1 drug such as cannabis can only be lawfully in the possession of constables and customs officers.

Lord Keith has said in this context: '. . .it is the duty of the custodian not to hand them back but to destroy them or to deliver them to a police officer so that they may be destroyed'.

(*R* v. *Maginnis* [1987] AC 303)

The lawful handling of controlled drugs

What are controlled drugs?

The large number of substances listed as controlled drugs range from dangerously addictive cocaine to humdrum and relatively harmless nitrazepam. The MDA regulations divide them into five schedules. Different classes of people may possess and supply controlled drugs according to the schedules. Anyone may possess and supply schedule 5 drugs but they are still (confusingly) listed as controlled drugs. Only those controlled drugs in schedules 2 and 3 of the MDA regulations are marked 'CD' in the British National Formulary. Nevertheless all five list controlled drugs for the diverse purposes of the criminal law. The five schedules are outlined below.

Schedule 1 substances

What are they?
They are, in general, controlled substances with no accepted therapeutic value such as cannabis, coca leaf, psilocin, and LSD.

Who may possess them?
Any controlled substance listed in all the schedules may be possessed by:
- a constable when acting in the course of his duty as such;
- a person engaged in conveying the drug to a person who may lawfully have that drug in his possession. . .';[2]
- persons granted a Home Office licence.

Anyone else in possession of the substances in schedule 1 is committing a crime. Emergency department staff may not possess them.

Drugs in schedules 2 and 3

What are they?
Schedule 2 contains the 'hard' drugs with therapeutic value, including cocaine, amphetamine, diamorphine, and most other strong opiates including methadone and codeine. Schedule 3 contains less potent therapeutic agents including buprenorphine and pentazocine.

Who may possess them?

Those who may **possess and supply** them include, among others:

- doctors, dentists and vets;
- pharmacists;
- sisters in charge of departments;
- nurses, and others acting under direction of a doctor or dentist.

The regulations also permit anyone to **possess** schedule 2 and 3 drugs under a practitioner's direction: '. . .a person may have in his possession any drug specified in schedule 2 or 3 for administration for medical, dental, or veterinary purposes In accordance with the directions of a practitioner. . .'[3] This means that patients may lawfully possess a drug prescribed for them and nursing staff and carers may administer it under the direction of a doctor or dentist.

However a person loses this exemption if he obtained the drugs improperly as by 'double scripting' (going to a second doctor and not disclosing his existing supply) or by obtaining the drugs dishonestly by making a false statement.

Schedule 4 and 5 drugs (minor drugs of abuse).

What are they?

Schedule 4 includes most benzodiazepines.

Schedule 5 includes very weak preparations of cocaine, opiates etc. from which it is difficult to extract amounts which are satisfactory for purposes of abuse.

Who may possess them?

Anyone may lawfully possess schedule 4 drugs provided they are in a 'medicinal product'. Anyone may also lawfully possess schedule 5 drugs.

Notification of and prescribing for addicts

Notification

The Misuse of Drugs Act s.10(2)(h) permits the Home Secretary to make regulations requiring a doctor to furnish particulars of any person he attends that he has reasonable grounds to suspect of being addicted to controlled drugs of any description.

Such regulations have been made[4] and notification to the Chief Medical Officer is required within 7 days. This may be done on special forms obtainable from the Chief Medical Officer which emergency departments should stock.

Prescribing

The Home Secretary may make regulations (under MDA s.10(2)(i)) prohibiting all doctors except those with special licences from prescribing certain drugs for addicts.

He has made these regulations[4] which permit only doctors with a Home Office licence to prescribe diamorphine, dipipanone ('dikes'), or cocaine to addicts. Any doctor may however prescribe these to relieve pain in anyone including addicts.

End notes

1. *Warner* v. *Metropolitan Police Commissioner* [1969] 2 AC 256
2. (reg 6(7)). The full list is:
   (a) a constable when acting in the course of his duty as such;
   (b) a person engaged in the business of a carrier when acting in the course of that business;
   (c) a person engaged in the business of the post office when acting in the course of that business;
   (d) an officer of Customs and Excise when acting in the course of his duty as such;
   (e) a person engaged in the work of any laboratory to which the drug has been sent for forensic examination when acting in the course of his duty as a person so engaged;
   (f) a person engaged in conveying the drug to a person who may lawfully have that drug in his possession.
3. Regulation 10(2)
4. Notification of and supply to addicts regulations 1973 (Statutory Instrument 1973 no. 799) amended by SI 1983 no. 1909

Further reading

British National Formulary (introductory pages)
Fortson, R. (1992) *The law on misuse of drugs and drug trafficking offences* (2nd ed.) Sweet and Maxwell.

CHAPTER 15

Mental health law

- **Compulsory powers over the mentally ill 149**
- **Treatment by the criminal courts 158**

Our great grandchildren will probably look upon contemporary psychiatric practice as being as primitive as we view that of the eighteenth and nineteenth centuries. However modest the progress in treatment for mental disorder it cannot be denied that the law, although imperfect, now permits a humane and respectful care of the afflicted.

The common law permitted the restraining of a dangerous lunatic.[1] Historical accounts describe degrading and inhuman imprisonment of patients. Private madhouses were the subject of judicial concern[2] and of the earliest mental health legislation.[3] Asylums were built in the nineteenth century mainly by charities or local authorities. Acts of Parliament regulated the conditions under which patients could be forced into them as well as their treatment within them. Mental illness was managed separately from physical illness until the start of the National Health Service in 1948. The facilities for the mentally ill, our methods of treatment and the approach to confinement have substantially changed in the second half of this century. Most patients are now out-patients, and most of the in-patients are voluntary. There remain a few purely mental hospitals, principally the secure units. It is now common for a general hospital to have a department of psychiatry.

The Mental Health Act of 1983 is the latest of a long series of mental health statutes and provides most of the powers to compel patients. It is the basis of the contemporary law regulating care of the mentally disordered. Codes of practice made under the Act have been laid before Parliament and, though not legally binding will be taken account of by a court. The most recent dates from 1993.

Legal position of the mentally ill

The law treats the mentally compromised differently in the following important areas:

(1) compulsory powers over admission, detention, and treatment in hospital;

(2) treatment by the criminal courts;

(3) ability to acquire and dispose of property and to make contracts.

The first two concern emergency department staff.

Compulsory powers over the mentally ill

As in all other areas of law, there are gaps and the available powers do not cover every situation.

'Sectioning' under the Mental Health Act

Sections 2,3, and 4 of the Mental Health Act 1983 enable a free person to be brought into hospital and kept there against his will. Sections 2 and 3 also enable medical treatment for mental illness to be given against the patient's will. These powers are brought into operation by the act of completing a form, provided a hospital agrees to accept the patient. Until the form is complete there is no power over that patient. This type of detention and treatment is supervised by the Mental Health Act Commissioners. Their importance in the preservation of the liberty of the subject is large. But for them, people could be deprived of their liberty without the benefit of any form of independent judicial consideration.

The sections

Section 2: compulsory admission for assessment (28 days)
An approved social worker or the nearest relative make the application. Two doctors must also recommend in writing that the patient:

'Is suffering from mental disorder of a nature or degree which warrants the detention. . .' **and**

'he ought to be so detained in the interests of his own health or safety **or** with a view to the protection of other persons'

'mental disorder' is defined in section 1(2) of the Mental Health Act 1983 as 'mental illness, arrested or incomplete development of mind, psychopathic disorder or any other disorder or disability of mind.' Section 1(3) in effect excludes from this: drug or alcohol dependence, sexual deviancy or promiscuity.

The only guidance from the courts has been illumination of the meaning of the words 'mental illness'. In 1974 Lord Justice Lawton said: 'The words are ordinary words of the English language. They have no particular medical significance. They have no particular legal significance'.

(*W* v. *L* [1974] QB 711)

Section 3: compulsory admission for treatment (6 months)
The application must be made by the patient's nearest relative or an approved social worker.[4] It then requires two doctors' written recommendation that the patient:

'is suffering from mental illness, severe mental impairment, psychopathic disorder or mental impairment and his mental disorder is of such a nature or degree which makes it appropriate for him to receive medical treatment in a hospital'; **and**

'in the case of psychopathic disorder or mental impairment, such treatment is likely to alleviate or prevent a deterioration of his condition'; **and**

'it is necessary for the health or safety of the patient **or** for the protection of other persons that he should receive such treatment and it cannot be provided unless he is detained. . .'

Section 4: emergency application for assessment (72 hours)
Either an approved social worker or the patient's nearest relative as well as one doctor must both state:

• that it is of urgent necessity for the patient to be detained under s.2, **and**

- that compliance (with the requirements of that section) would involve undesirable delay.

Otherwise the grounds for admission are the same as for s.2. This application can be 'upgraded' into a section 2 application by receiving the second medical recommendation within 72 hours.

The Code of Practice discourages the use of this section except in genuine emergency and it should not be used in place of the section 2 procedure merely for administrative convenience.

The doctors

For sections 2 and 3, one of the two doctors must be an approved specialist in mental disorder. One or other of the doctors should be acquainted with the patient. Only one of the doctors may generally be on the staff of the admitting NHS hospital.

The emergency section 4 application requires only one medical recommendation and the doctor need not be an approved specialist but should if possible have previous acquaintance with the patient.

Treatment without consent

Most forms of treatment for mental disorder may be given without consent to a patient detained under either section 2 or 3.[5] This includes necessary physical treatment such as life saving medical treatment after a suicide attempt or the tube feeding or an anorexic. Note that the 'emergency' section 4 gives no power to impose treatment without consent[6] which is a considerable disadvantage.

B was a compulsory in-patient under section 3. She starved herself to 35 kg and required tube feeding. She applied to the court to prevent this being done by the hospital. She was unsuccessful.

The court held that 'medical treatment' could be given to a patient admitted under section 2 or 3 if it was to 'alleviate or prevent a deterioration of the mental disorder' or 'ancillary acts which prevented the patient harming herself or which alleviated the symptoms of the disorder'.

Lord Justice Hoffman said: 'It would seem to me strange

> if a hospital could, without the patient's consent, give him treatment directed to alleviating a psychopathic disorder showing itself in suicidal tendencies but not, without such consent, be able to treat the consequences of a suicide attempt. In my judgement the term "medical treatment . . . for the mental disorder" in s.63 includes such ancillary acts. . .'
>
> 'The case of *Re C* in which a schizophrenic was held entitled to refuse treatment for gangrene is distinguishable. The gangrene was entirely unconnected with the mental disorder'.
>
> (*B* v. *Croydon Health Authority* [1995] 2 WLR 294, citing *Re C*. [1994] 1 All ER 819)

In-patients

Both doctors and nurses have certain holding power over an in-patient as described in section 5. These powers apply only to in-patients and cannot be exercised in emergency departments.

The doctor's power

A patient already in hospital for any reason may be detained for 72 hours if a report is furnished to the hospital managers by the doctor in charge of his treatment or by one other doctor he has nominated. The report must state that it appears to him that such an application 'ought to be made'.

It enables a patient to be detained for a proper assessment for section 2 or section 3 admission but does not enable treatment without consent.

The nurse's power

A patient in hospital for the treatment of mental disorder may be detained for six hours once a written note has been made by an approved registered mental nurse that:

• he is suffering from such mental disorder that he must immediately be restrained from leaving;

• for his own health or safety or for the protection of others;

• the doctor cannot come in time to exercise his holding power.

Out-patients: guardianship application
On application with two medical recommendations, a
guardian, usually the local authority, can be appointed over a
patient (section 7). The legal effect of this is minimal save that
an absconder can be returned to the place of residence
required by the guardian. It does not enable treatment to be
given without consent. Recently, following several murders,
there has been criticism of the lack of effective compulsion of
out-patients.

Removal to a place of safety

By warrant (section 135)
A constable accompanied by an approved social worker and a
doctor can enter specified premises with a warrant and take a
person to a place of safety. The warrant is issued by a magistrate on application by an approved social worker, if the magistrate suspects a person:

- is suffering from mental disorder, **and**

- is being ill-treated, neglected, or out of control, **or**

- is unable to care for himself and living alone.

By arrest in a public place (section 136)
A constable who finds a person in a place to which the public
has access who appears to be

- suffering from mental disorder **and**

- in immediate need of care and control

may, in the interests of that person or the protection of others,
remove him to a place of safety. He may be detained at the
place of safety for 72 hours for an application for compulsory
admission or for making other arrangements for his care.

'*place of safety*'
This means:[7]
(a) social services' residential accommodation
(b) any health service hospital[8]
(c) a police station
(d) a mental nursing home
(e) a residential home for the mentally disordered
(f) any other suitable place if the occupier is willing.

The code of practice points out the identification of preferred places of safety is a matter for local agreement.

Powers to detain the patient at the place of safety
If he escapes he can be retaken by the person who had his custody immediately before the escape or by any constable or approved social worker.[9]

Treatment
There is no power to impose any form of treatment without the patient's consent during detention in the place of safety.

Who should detain the patient?
The Mental Health Act places no obligation on hospital staff to restrain or imprison any patient unless they are unwise enough to take over from police the custody of an arrested patient. They then not only acquire the power to retrieve him if he leaves[9] but probably also owe a legal duty of care to him and any potential victims to prevent his escape.

The Code of Practice recommends that a clear local policy be agreed between social services, district health authority, NHS trust, and the Chief Officer of Police. This policy should in particular define:

(1) the responsibility of police to remain with the patient for his health or safety or the protection of others; and

(2) If the patient is not admitted the responsibility of police, doctors, and approved social workers for the patient's safe return to the community.

Common law powers

(powers over a mentally disordered patient who has not been 'sectioned')
Every emergency department is familiar with the difficult situation where a patient appears mentally disordered but refuses treatment for self harm or threatens to leave or to harm himself.

In general, treatment cannot be imposed on a competent adult without his consent. Even though 'sectionably' insane he remains legally competent to consent to or refuse treatment provided he is still capable of understanding the broad nature of the treatment. Once a section 2 or section 3 application is completed he can be restrained and treated for his mental

illness and its physical consequences. And if he is in a place of
safety under section 135 or 136 he can be restrained by those
with custody of him. But the majority of apparently mentally
disordered patients will not be under any kind of 'section' and
the Mental Health Act has nothing to say about them!
There is a duty to take reasonable care of such patients but
only to take such measures as are lawful. Any illegal restraint
or treatment is assault and battery and if staff are injured in
the process, they have only themselves to blame.[10] Whatever
compulsory powers staff may have over such a patient can
only stem from case law.

Is there power of restraint at Common Law?
The nature and scope of such a power, if it exists at all, is far
from certain. Delving into the reported cases throws up mere
shadows of the ancient law and anyway is only in the form of
indirect references to it by the judges.
    In *Brookshaw* v. *Hopkins*, Lord Mansfield remarked 'God
forbid, too, that a man should be punished for restraining the
fury of a lunatic, when that is the case.'
((1790) Lofft 240)
    In 1846 in *Shuttleworth's* case the Lord Chief Justice asked
'Is not the confining of a dangerous lunatic also founded on
common law principles?'. Mr Justice Earle stated further on:
'. . .(the Lunacy Act) . . . is not a general prohibition against
confining lunatics. That is left as at common law.'
((1846) 9 QB 651)
    In *Fletcher* v. *Fletcher* it was held that 'by the common law
of England no person can be imprisoned as a lunatic unless he
is actually insane at the time'.
((1859) 1 EI &EI 420)
    In 1862 a judge said a surgeon would be justified in restrain-
ing a 'dangerous lunatic in such a state it was likely he would
do mischief to anyone'.
(*Scott* v. *Wakem* (1862) 3 F & F 327)
    However in 1863 Lord Chief Justice Cockburn commented
that 'a plea of justification would have been abundantly established' by two doctors sued for forcibly treating a woman for
delirium tremens. This was not in issue in the case since the
doctors had not claimed their action was justified but that she
had consented. Lord Cockburn went on to refer to 'the power

which the law gave to medical men' and to 'this noble profession'. This special power of doctors does not make any reappearance in the law reports!

(*Symm* v. *Fraser* (1863) 3 F & F 859)

There are few other cases on the subject. It would seem therefore that the Common Law permits the restraint only of a 'dangerous lunatic' who must actually be insane at that time. The use of these words obviously has changed but their meaning is still clear.

Guidance from the Code of Practice

The Code of Practice (at pp. 58–59) more or less agrees with this statement of the law but does so in its own less concise language:

The terms of this advice imply that it applies to 'sectionable' mentally disordered people who are dangerous.

'On rare occasions involving emergencies, where it is not possible immediately to apply the provisions of the Mental Health Act, a patient suffering from a mental disorder which is leading to behaviour that is an immediate serious danger to himself or to other people may be given such treatment as represents the minimum necessary response to avert that danger.

It must be emphasised that the administration of such treatment is not an alternative to giving treatment under the Mental Health Act nor should its administration delay the proper application of the Act to the patient at the earliest opportunity.'

Limit of the Common Law power

The power arising from case law does not extend further than stated above. There are two appeal cases in which, if it had existed, a common law power in excess of this could have been pleaded. It was not pleaded in either case. Had such a power existed and been pleaded it would have reversed the outcome of both.

Case 1

> The officer in command of a military base believed the plaintiff was a dangerous lunatic and placed him under house arrest for three days so that two medical officers could assess him. The doctors did not pronounce him a lunatic. The Judicial Committee of the Privy Council (equivalent to the House of Lords) held that the plaintiff was entitled to damages for false imprisonment. They said: 'There is no law which authorises the police . . . or an officer in command, . . . in consequence of a bona fide belief that a person is dangerous by reason of actual lunacy, to put him in confinement in order that he may be visited and examined by medical officers and to keep him in confinement until such officers can feel themselves justified in reporting whether the person is a dangerous lunatic or not'.
>
> (*Sinclair* v. *Broughton and the Government of India* (1882) 47 LT 170)

Case 2

> A doctor, two policemen and another were attempting to 'section' the patient and entered his house. The doctor had not yet examined him but was preparing a sedative injection when a policeman (called John Major) went to restrain him. The patient thought the policeman was about to strike him and he punched the officer breaking his nose. The patient was convicted of assault occasioning actual bodily harm. He appealed successfully. The Lord Chief Justice (Lord Parker) said 'since the application form was not at the time duly completed by the addition of Dr Hardman's medical certificate, none of those persons had any lawful authority to restrain the patient and convey him to hospital. Indeed they were trespassers . . . I cannot say that to hit out with the fist is an unreasonable use of force.'
>
> (*Townley* v. *Rushworth* (1963) 62 LGR 95)

Treatment by the criminal courts

Mental disorder and criminal responsibility

This is relevant because emergency departments can be the scene of bad behaviour by visitors, obstructing the care of patients and demoralizing staff. Although such behaviour may be criminal, few attempts seem to be made to secure punishment of it in a general belief that any form of mental illness or intoxication by drugs or alcohol will cause it to be excused by a court. Such things may be taken into account in imposing a sentence but their use in escaping conviction is decidedly limited.

The elements of a crime
For a person to be convicted it must be proved both that

(1) the offender did the unlawful act (the *actus reus*) and

(2) he had the appropriate mental element (the *mens rea*).

The mental element is specific to each offence and may require intention, recklessness, negligence[11] or, rarely, blameless ignorance.[12]

Defences associated with mental health
An accused person escapes conviction if either the *actus reus* or the *mens rea* are not proved. One way of attaining this is by raising the defence of automatism which in effect denies the unlawful act by saying it was not voluntary. Another way is by the defence of intoxication which may negate the necessary mental element in certain crimes in which the prosecution is required to prove specific intent or knowledge on the part of the defendant. If either of these defences succeeds the result is acquittal.

The defence of insanity is different. If proved it results in a special verdict of 'Not guilty by reason of insanity.'[13] This is not an acquittal and the court has wide powers to deal with the offender including ordering indefinite incarceration in a special hospital.

On a charge of murder, the accused may instead be convicted of manslaughter on grounds of diminished responsibility. This is a defence much wider in its ambit than that of insanity but is only available in murder cases.[14]

The defence of insanity

This is a narrow legal concept, not a medical one. Its meaning was defined by the judges in 1843 in the M'Naghten Rules: '. . .to establish a defence on the ground of insanity it must be clearly proved that, at the time of the committing of the act, the party accused was labouring under such a defect of reason, from disease of the mind, as not to know the nature and quality of the act he was doing, or, if he did know it, that he did not know he was doing what was wrong.'

'*disease of the mind*'

'Mind' is used in the ordinary sense of the mental faculties of reason, memory, and understanding.[15] 'Disease' is not limited to mental illness in the psychiatric sense but can also be physical such as arteriosclerosis, epilepsy, brain tumour, or diabetes. It cannot be due to an 'external factor' such as cerebral concussion, alcohol, drugs, or insulin induced hypoglycaemia.

Lord Denning has said:
'The major mental diseases, which the doctors call psychoses, such as schizophrenia, are clearly diseases of the mind'

(*Bratty* v. *A-G for Northern Ireland* [1963] AC 386, [1961] 3 All ER 523)

'*defect of reason*'

failure to use powers of reason is not insanity. Neither is lack of control over emotions or an irresistible impulse.

'*nature and quality of the act*'

This refers to the physical nature and quality of the act, not its moral or legal quality.

'*did not know he was doing what was wrong*'

This means he was not aware it was forbidden either morally or by the law.

It must be apparent that the defence of insanity requires very severe mental dysfunction. It may be raised by the prosecution, the defence, or the judge. Until 1957 it saved offenders from the rope.[14] It is now used to protect society from recurrence of their dangerous conduct.

The defence of automatism

> 'This quagmire of law, seldom entered nowadays save by those in desperate need of some kind of defence'
>
> (*Lord Justice Lawton in R* v. *Quick and Paddison* [1973] 3 All ER 347 (CA))

To be a crime an act must be one of voluntary willed conduct. If there is a total destruction of voluntary control, but not due to 'disease of the mind', the act does not constitute a crime because the accused person was in a state of automatism. Impaired or reduced control is not enough.[16] The act must be completely involuntary and is confined to acts done by a person who is not conscious of what he is doing or by spasms, reflex actions, and convulsions.[17]

The distinction between automatism and insanity is that 'disease of the mind' or insanity is due to an internal factor while automatism is due to an external factor such as an attack by a swarm of bees, cerebral concussion, hypnosis, an anaesthetic, drugs taken under medical direction, or hypoglycaemia due to insulin.[18] The defence of automatism will not be allowed if it was self-inflicted or the accused person was reckless in, for example, his failure to take regular meals while on insulin.

It can be seen that automatism is a narrow legal concept like that of insanity. However while insanity has to be proved, automatism does not. The prosecution have the burden of proving an act was voluntary. Once sufficient medical

> A diabetic failed to take sufficient food and committed an assault causing grievous bodily harm. His defence of automatism failed.
> (*R* v. *Bailey* [1983] 2 All ER 503)

evidence has been adduced to raise the issue of automatism, the defendant will be acquitted unless the prosecution do show the act was voluntary.

The defence of intoxication

The law is surprisingly firm on this subject, placing the safety of the public above concern for the offender. It is well recognized that a person is more likely to lose control of himself and commit offences when intoxicated and this does not excuse him at all.

Essentially no defence
Subject to the exceptions below, it is no defence to a criminal charge to have been drunk or intoxicated by drugs at the time of the offence. Furthermore, if an accused person puts intoxication forward as part of a defence at his trial, the prosecution is then absolved from proving the necessary mental element of the offence.

> Lord Elwyn-Jones said 'whenever . . .the offence with which the accused is charged is manslaughter or assault at common law or the statutory offence of unlawful wounding under s.20 or of assault occasioning actual bodily harm under s.47 of the Offences against the Person Act 1861, . . . it is no excuse in law that, because of drink or drugs which the accused himself had taken knowingly and willingly, he had deprived himself of the ability to exercise self-control, to realise the possible consequences of what he was doing or even to be conscious that he was doing it . . . the jury may be properly instructed that they "can ignore the subject of drink or drugs as being in any way a defence to" charges of this character'.
>
> (*DPP* v. *Majewski* [1977] AC 443, [1976] 2 All ER 142 (HL)

Exceptions

A crime of 'specific intent'
Certain crimes require a mental element which is purposive and needs something more than mere contemplation of the

prohibited act and foresight of its consequences. A state of intoxication may render the accused incapable of forming the required intent. In that case the mental element may fail to be proved and he will be acquitted.[19] This is not the same as loss of self control due to drink or drugs. The following is a list of common crimes of this character.

murder,

wounding or causing grievous bodily harm with intent,

theft,

robbery,

burglary with intent to steal,

handling stolen goods,

endeavouring to obtain money on a forged cheque

certain cases of criminal damage

certain indecent assaults with indecent purpose,

an attempt at any crime of specific intent.

A man taking an LSD trip was burdened by the unfortunate misapprehension he was fighting snakes at the centre of the earth and he killed a fellow tripper by hitting her head and cramming a sheet into her mouth. He was charged with murder and accordingly convicted of manslaughter.

(R v. *Lipman* [1970] 1 QB 152, [1969] 3 All ER 410 (CA))

Involuntary intoxication
If a person is given alcohol or drugs without his knowledge it may be used to show he was incapable of forming the necessary mental element of any kind of offence at all. This may apply when his soft drink is spiked with alcohol but not if he simply underestimated the amount or effect of what he took voluntarily. Again, this does not excuse simple loss of control.

Medical direction
Intoxication due to drugs taken in accordance with medical direction can amount to automatism (see above).

A man took diazepam tablets then set his girlfriend's flat on fire. On appeal, his conviction for this offence was quashed because he claimed to be under the influence of a 'soporific' drug and that made all the difference. With a 'soporific' drug the prosecution were still obliged to prove the mental element of the offence.

This was a surprising finding of the Court of Appeal. The judges seem to have relied on their own knowledge and said: 'Valium is wholly different in kind from drugs which are liable to cause unpredictability or aggressiveness'. 'The drug was soporific, unlike alcohol or dangerous drugs'.

(*R* v. *Hardie* [1985] 1 WLR 64)

There may now be a series of cases determining which drugs are 'intoxicating' and which are not. It may be that those who illegally take sedative drugs will be in a similar position to those with self-inflicted automatism where it matters whether they were reckless as to the drug's effect when they took it.

End notes

1. *Scott* v. *Wakem* (1862) 3 F & F 327
2. *R* v. *Coate*, the keeper of a madhouse (1772) Lofft 73
3. Act for Regulating Madhouses 1774
4. If the nearest relative objects, the social worker must obtain approval of the county court
5. Mental Health Act 1983 s.63
6. Mental Health Act 1983 s.56
7. Mental Health Act 1983 s.135(6)
8. Mental Health Act 1983 s.145(1)
9. Mental Health Act 1983 s.138
10. *Townley* v. *Rushworth* (1963) 62 LGR 95
11. e.g. as in careless driving
12. e.g. as in certain sexual offences involving girls under 16 where the accused does not suspect their age
13. Trial of Lunatics Act 1883, s.2(1) (as amended)
14. The defence of diminished responsibility was created by the Homicide Act of 1957.

164 • Mental health law

15. *Lord Diplock in R* v. *Sullivan* [1983] 2 All ER 673
16. Attorney-General's Reference (No 2 of 1992) [1993] 3 WLR 982
17. Lord Denning in *Bratty* v. *Attorney General for Northern Ireland* [1963] AC 386, [1961] 3 All ER 523 (HL)
18. *R* v. *Quick and Paddison* [1973] 3 All ER 347 (CA)
19. *DPP* v. *Beard* [1920] AC 479

Further reading

Hoggett, B. *Mental Health Law* Sweet and Maxwell
Smith and Hogan, *Criminal Law;* Butterworths

Index

165